Thomas Wright

The Acid Sisters and other Poems

Thomas Wright

The Acid Sisters and other Poems

ISBN/EAN: 9783744711418

Printed in Europe, USA, Canada, Australia, Japan

Cover: Foto ©Thomas Meinert / pixelio.de

More available books at **www.hansebooks.com**

The Acid Sisters,

and other Poems.

By THOMAS WRIGHT,

Author of "The Life of William Cowper," "The Town
of Cowper," "The Life of Daniel Defoe," " The
Mystery of St. Dunstan's," &c., &c.

OLNEY:
Thomas Wright,
1897.

PREFACE.

OF the poems that form the present Volume, some have already appeared in "The Sketch," "The Literary World," and other periodicals. My affection for the Literature of Ancient Greece and Rome has led me to place "The Lost Masterpieces" in the foreground; the longest poem, however, and the one that gives the name to the collection, is "The Acid Sisters," a mediæval love story. For the sonnet on page 50 I had the honour to be thanked by Her Majesty the Queen. The lines on page 85 owe their origin to the kindness of the Rev. J. P. Langley, who lent the slides referred to. It gives me great pleasure also to be able to express my indebtedness to Alfred Austin, Esq., the Poet Laureate, for so kindly allowing the work to be dedicated to him, and for interesting himself in a volume of verse emanating, to use his own expression, from a spot sanctified by the recollection of the pious breath of William Cowper.

THOMAS WRIGHT.

COWPER SCHOOL, OLNEY.
    21st March, 1897.

CONTENTS.

SUBJECTS FROM ANCIENT HISTORY.

POEMS RELATING TO OLNEY AND VICINITY.

Miscellaneous Poems.

Poems from my Novels.

POEMS ADDRESSED TO FRIENDS.

POEMS WRITTEN FOR MY SCHOLARS.

THE LOST MASTERPIECES OF THE WORLD.

I.—LITERATURE.

An immense amount of splendid literature is lost to us. Of the seventy tragedies of Æschylus we possess only seven, and Sophocles and Euripides have also suffered terribly. Sappho is represented by a few fragments, Livy by thirty-five books out of one hundred and forty-two, whilst of one writer of distinction, who wrote more than two hundred tragedies, we possess only a few lines.

I CAME upon a treasure
   One stilly winter night,
Too vast for man to measure,
   So rich it dimmed my sight ;
   Said I, " It dims my sight,
Oh, shall I have the leisure
   To gather up my right,
Or lose one half the pleasure ! "

Some African empiric
   Had hoarded in this crypt
Song, play and book satiric
   That Time had filched or clipt,
   That wasteful Time had clipt ;
And many a long lost lyric
   Of Sappho here I lipped
Too fine for panegyric.

As unto scented flowers
   Surrender restless bees,
I lost myself for hours
   With rich Euripides ;
   Above Euripides
His vanished labour towers,
   I drank as thirsty trees
Delicious pattering showers.

Euripides.--Four syllables, accent on second.

A

Stood all the odes of Pindar   ·
    With nothing mutilated,
And Livy's books to tinder
    Long burnt were re-instated ;
    And, Livy re-instated,
No gap was left to hinder
    My studies.—Re-created
For me from ash and cinder

Were Æschylus and Sophocles ;
    In Pindar's chair of iron
I sat, and read the melodies
    Of pasture-loving Bion,
    The melodies of Bion,
And when I turned from these
    ' Twas to the glorious Chian *
And van ·.ished Odysseys.

And yet as I was reading
    All quiet in my chair,
I felt the scene receding.
    " I dream," in my dispair,
    I cried, in my dispair,
Then, supplicating, pleading,
    " Permit," arose my prayer,
" I may not wake ; 'tis feeding
    On manna caught in air."

But vain was the petition,
    The words were hardly spoken.
When crumbled my munition,
    My secret crypt was broken,
    And Pindar's chair was broken;
Of all the erudition
    And song remained no token,
And yet there was fruition ;

For sometimes an ecstatic
    Rare glow comes over me,
And garlands aromatic
    On altars fair I see,
    An eastern sunset see
With changing hues prismatic,
And hear some long lost Attic
    Or Dorian melody.

* Homer.

I thereupon remember
    Some passage I had read
That evening in December,
    Among the mighty dead,—
    Among the glorious dead,
The spoil of fire and ember,
    And knife and dust of ages ;
That evening I remember
    When, face to face with sages,
    And bards, I read those pages
That memorable December.

Telemachus* descended
    To Pluto ; Paul arose
To Heavenly Regions splendid,
    But neither might disclose,
    Oh, neither might disclose
The great uncomprehended !
    Injunctions, too, that close
The lip, my boon attended :
But I through regions splendid
    Have passed that no man knows.

2.—PAINTING.

If the great writers of ancient times have suffered, the painters have suffered more. All the masterpieces that were the wonder and pride of Greece have perished.

THE swollen stream was sobbing,
    " Had but the night one star ! "
I said.—" To wait is robbing
    Thy soul," I heard afar.—
Said I, " The stream is sobbing,
    The plash and darkness bar,
The night has not one star,
    I cannot still this throbbing."

" Yet come ! "—Said I, " Appalling "
    Is this—the water's lap
Is echoed, not the calling,
    Weird voice ; dread things will hap—
Terrific things will hap,"
    (And still the voice kept calling)
" These echoes and the wrap
    Nigrescent are appalling ! "

* Telemachus.—Four syllables, accent on second.

"Take slave, thy manumission,"
   I heard.   "Thy fears have piled
New woes on woes ; submission
   Befits thee as a child."
I followed as a child,
Surceased the mind's attrition.
   Said I, " The current wild
Is passed, reveal thy mission' "

But scarcely had I uttered
   The words unto my sprite,
When from my eyes there fluttered
   The ebon scales of night—
The atramentous night
Spread wing.   Some magic muttered
   Had wrought a blaze of light,
And I was in my shuttered
   Enchanted crypt.   The sight
Transfixed.   Then my magician :—
" Thou saidst, ' Reveal thy mission,"
   Ah, memorable night !

And was my temple hoary
   The same yet not the same ;
The walls with Grecian story
   And scene were all aflame,
   With pictures all aflame
By master souls, the glory
   Of Greece.   Ah, honoured name !
Great Nicias* told the story
   Of Io's fall and shame.

See dazzling Aphrodite †
   Arising from the sea,
That loveliness is mighty—
   Hath ever mastery—
The fair Campaspe‡ knew,
The fragrant slave-girl knew,
The gift of king to king.
The Coan painter king

---

* Nicias painted pictures of Io, Ulysses invoking the Shades of the Dead,
and Nemea sitting on a lion.

   Apelles, born at Cos, hence the epithet Coan, was presented by Alexander
the Great with a beautiful slave, Campaspe, whose charms were transferred to
Aphrodite, whom Apelles depicted arising from the foam.

   ‡ Campaspe.   Three syllables, accent on second.

   † Aphrodite.   Four syllables, accent on third.

No rival knew in man,
And poets as the peerless sing
The Macedonian.

And Cimon's beauteous sister
Once more approached to us
From out a plane tree vista
In robe diaphanous,
The robe diaphanous
That round her form she threw
When Polygnotus[1] drew
Her blinding charms for us,
And showed the blue veins through.

Some Centaurs,[2] and below them
Their names—archaic plan—
That every one might know them;
Stood here the herd-god Pan,
The hirsute poet Pan,
With pipes prepared to blow them;
The picture Ælian
Belauds, to which Protogenes[3]
(Resolved his darling work should please)
Seven precious cycles grew,
The moistened-lupine eater who
What time the sponge ire-pinioned flew
Surceased his threnodies.

On shrines and gods and bowers,
I gaze, and gaze, and gaze;
The minutes grew to hours,
The hours to rapturous days.
To swift eventful days—
When lo! before these bowers
And gods arose a haze.
A voice exclaimed, " 'Tis over; let
The scene dissolve. The bounds are set."
"Not yet," I cried, distressed, "not yet!"

1 Polygnotus (Four syllables, accent on third), introduced into his pictures
Elpinice, the sister of Cimon.

2 Painted by Zeuxis.

3 Protogenes (Four syllables, accent on second). This painter, unable to
represent, to his satisfaction, the foam at the mouth of a dog, flew into a
temper, and flung a sponge at the picture. This gave the desired effect.

Then from my dream I wakened,
  But when I close my eyes
I see again before me
  Each spell-producing prize ;
Apelles comes before me,
  I see again the glister
Of Juno's gemmy car,
  Come Cimon's lovely sister
From where the planes afar,
  Extend adown the vista,

The buskined Delian Dian
  That Nichomachus drew,*
And who the Nemean Lion,
  And who the Gorgons slew.
I may should sweet life flow on
  My children's children see,
But will the kingly Coan
  Again appear to me !
  Shall I his pictures see
  Again ? It cannot be.
But I with the Golden-garlanded,
In whom Apollo's ichor sped,
And him, and earth's most glorious dead
  Have been in company.

* Nichomachus (Four syllables, accent on third).
The Gorgons. Three terrible hags slain by Perseus.
The Coan.—Apelles (Three syllables, accent on second).
  The Golden-garlanded. The painter Parrhasius wore a golden garland.
He declared himself to be descended from Apollo.
  The author hopes sometime to write a Third Part "Sculpture."

SUBJECTS FROM ENGLISH LITERATURE.

COWPER AND BURNS.

ONE bright morning in a brew-house,
  Back against a mighty cask,
Burns, of all around forgetful,
  Sat enjoying Cowper's " Task."
All the time in Weston spinnie
  Under fragrant foliage,
William Cowper wandered poring
  Over Burns's deathless page.

Each a genius in the other
  Recognised, and bard of grit,
Friend to man and beast, as brother,
  Artist, humorist and wit.

Pleasant thought, that Burns in fancy
  Could in Weston spinnie stand,
Seat himself in Cowper's parlour,
  Taste his tea, and grasp his hand.

And that Cowper should have tittered
  Over Tam o'Shanter's plight,
Seen the " Cotter's " guileless circle
  Gathered round the " Book " at night.

Still more pleasing the reflection,
  Swallow-like it oft returns,
That while Burns was reading Cowper
  Cowper was absorbed in Burns.

16th September, 1896.

THE MAN FROM PORLOCK.

Whilst engaged upon "Kubla Khan" Coleridge was unfortunately " called out by a person on business from Porlock, and detained half an hour." On his return the inspiration had fled, and the most seductive poetical fragment in the language was never again touched.

" Of the blacklegs of this yeasty ball
   Which do you most abhor ? "—
" Well, John of England, callous Paul [1]
   Of Rome, and several more ·
Hateful as vampire, ghoul or warlock,"—
" But how about the man from Porlock ? "

" Thus in the family of Hare
   Or Burke [2] I should not care to marry,
And skittish manners marked our spare,
   Meek celibate, the Tudor Harry ;
There's Bluebeard with his key and door-lock."
" But how about the man from Porlock ? "

" In Cæsar Borgia I could see
   Nothing attractive : neither hero
Nor saint was John of Muscovy ; [3]
   I do not feel much drawn to Nero—
A reprobate from foot to forelock."—
But how about the man from Porlock ? "

GLORIOUS JOHN.

" Will's Coffee House," Russell Street, Covent Garden, was a famous resort of wits and poets. The leading spirit of this brilliant coterie was the poet Dryden, often called " Glorious John.''

Fill a glass to " Glorious John."
   Not of wine, I do not drink it,
There are rills on Helicon,
   Into Aganippe* sink it.

Classic " Wills " of old Cockaigne
   Looms with balcony before us,
Wit and poet meet again,
   Ripple epigram and chorus.

1 Pope Paul IV., Organiser of the Inquisition.
2 Burke and Hare, Murderers. Burke was hanged 28th Jan. 1829.
3 John of Muscovy : Ivan IV. of Russia, The Terrible.
* Aganippe. (Four syllables, accent on third).

Dryden, seated on his throne,
Ode and sonnet criticises,
Condescends to read his own,
Snuffs the frankincense that rises.

Reverence he provokes and fear,
Ably rules his loyal nation,
Boisterously his friends we cheer,
Greet his foes with ululation.

Hostile bards we castigate,
Who would spare an anaconda !
On our oracle we wait,
All his sage pronouncements ponder.

Should the gracious monarch pass
Snuff-box with its fragrant powder,
Glow we like to burnished brass,
Boast like Niobe,[1] but louder.

In our ode if he discover
Beauties, pipe our hearts like finches,
We are happier than a lover,
Taller grow by several inches.

But should he with changed demeanour
On a rival praise bestow,
We with jealousy are greener
Than a polished peridot.[2]

Homage none around denied him
As enthroned at " Wills " he sat,
Seemed all other kings beside him
Petty as a calicrat.[3]

Raise the crystal from the spring
Limbecked out of Helicon,
Drink, and let your plaudits ring
Loud to great and glorious John !

28th October, 1896.

---

1 Niobe. Three syllables, accent on first.
2 Peridot. A precious stone. The last letter is silent.
3 Calicrat. Old name for the ant. Calicrates used to carve ants, etc., in ivory.

WHEN JOSEPH REIGNED AT "BUTTON'S."

What "Will's" was to Dryden, "Button's" Coffee House, Great Russell Street, became to Joseph Addison, the famous author of the Roger De Coverley and other papers in the "Spectator."

WHEN Joseph reigned at ' Button's '
The world was not polite,
To call clear Pope and classic
An ass discloses spite ;   .
As Dennis[1] did—
John Dennis—
How could you !

To dub Defoe of Crusoe fame
An idiot and a dunce,
Doth shock ; yet, caustic Dr. Swift,[2]
You said it more than once ;
You know you did.
Oh ! Jonathan,
How could you !

It seems that Swift no tongue so well
As Billingsgate could use ;
That argue worse no mortal could,
And better none abuse.
You said that—
Oh ! D. Defoe,
How could you !

And one threw down the curtained wall
Of Lady Mary's room,[3]
And showed her ere she used her comb
Her powder and perfume.
Pope did that,
Oh ! ' A. P. E.,' *
How could you !

1 John Dennis the distinguished critic.

2 Swift, the author of Gulliver's Travels.

3 Lady Mary Montagu. After Pope quarrelled with her he satirised her under the name of Sappho.

* It was Dennis who good-naturedly pointed out that the initials and last letter of Pope's name spelt Ape.

Sir Richard Steele was not exempt
From like malign attacks;
We're told he drank, but, really, were
His morals quite so lax
As Hoadly said ?[1]
Right reverend sir,
How could you!

King Joseph even was not spared :
It seems he had not sung
Without two hundred pounds a year
To lubricate his tongue—
You said that,
Oh, D. Defoe,
How could you!

Indeed we're shocked, and justly shocked,
At every one and all;
For with examples such as yours,
We moderns well may fall.
Whatever else we take from you,
To ape your manners would not do ;
No, not at all, at all.

THE MEETING OF COLERIDGE AND KEATS.

How swiftly as the eve draws nigh
The sun goes down. 'Twas set
Or almost when in yonder lane
A slender youth we met,
Who soon had entered man's estate,
We leaned against that lichened gate.

'Twas Keats. There slid a word or two
Between us, scarcely more,
I had not as I recollect,
E'er seen the boy before ;
His open face, but dreamy eye,
Attracted me, I knew not why.

1 Hoadly, Dr. Hoadly, Bishop of Winchester, d. 1761.

He left us, then returned again,
　And as my face he scanned,
" I wish to have the memory
　Of having pressed your hand,
Nor Coleridge, will you decline,"
He said, and placed his palm on mine.

But when I felt its touch, there came
　On me an icy breath,
And I soliloquised, " Within
　That gelid hand is death."
But Heaven decreed that first those white,
Thin fingers crystal verse should write.

" Endymion " and the " Grecian Urn "
　Were penned our fields amid,
And then he passed from us.　He lies
　By Cestius' pyramid.
So young ! Yet dry the falling tear,
For Shelley's spirit hovers near.

　　　　　　　9*th, October,* 1896.

THE REVEREND LAWRENCE STERNE.

Author of " Tristram Shandy " published 1760-7, creator of the world-famous
characters Uncle Toby and Widow Wadman.

' Tis understood that two or three
　Confess with some concern
They do not quite know how to take
　The Reverend Lawrence Sterne.

When gentlemen who should adore
　Their wives to others turn
We cry—it's *a la mode* to cry—
　" Oh, Reverend Lawrence Sterne ! "

And there are pages here and there
　That one might wisely burn,
A pair of scissors much improves
　The Reverend Lawrence Sterne.

Upon the very lowest shelves
　To which the children turn
We've squeezed some scores of books ; but not
　The Reverend Lawrence Sterne.

From Burton * and the earlier wits
　He stole without concern,
Nor made the least acknowledgment.
　Fie ! Reverend Lawrence Sterne.

But Uncle Toby several sins
　That scald, and eat, and burn,
Has covered ;—almost : anctified—
　The Reverend Lawrence Sterne.

In all the Shandies and in Trim
　Much goodness we discern,
And feel that some was part of thee
　O Reverend Lawrence Sterne.

And Widow Wadman ! Could the soul
　For choicer pictures yearn !
They must—'tis certain they reflect
　The Reverend Lawrence Sterne.

And if my books I were compelled—
　Say all save six—to burn,
I think among the six I'd set
　The Reverend Lawrence Sterne.

7th Dec. 1896.

"ERINNA"

OR, ALEXANDER POPE AND WILLIAM COWPER.

WHEN ladies wrecked susceptive hearts,
　Time gone, or badly battered them,
The poets called them fancy names,
　And toasted, rhymed and flattered them.

˙ So Pope of Judith Cowper sang
　In Twickenham's grotto shady,
And still the curious may read
　The " Letters to a Lady."

But when by strings of lovers thronged,
　She singled one and married,
The poet's laudatory rhymes
　Were to a rival carried.

* Robert Burton, author of The Anatomy of Melancholy, d. 1639. Sterne d. 1768.

But scarce was she from one bard free,
　Ere straight against another
She ran—the child whose prattle cheered
　Her grave and reverend brother.[1]

And she, whose lips susceptive Pope
　Had praised but never tasted,
Upon a bard in leading strings
　Deliberately wasted.

Oh, why will lovely ladies dole
　(Will no-one objurgate them ?)
Their honied favours unto those
　Who can't appreciate them!

But Pope's Erinna! May we not
　Among the happy group her—
Allied by bond of love to Pope,
　By bond of kin to Cowper.[2]

　　　　　　　　17th Sept. 1896.

THE TWO DEFOES.

Daniel Defoe, the great Novelist...............Died 1731, aged 71.
Daniel Defoe, " The last of the Defoes " Died 1896, aged 22.

ONE in San Francisco sleeps,
　One at home. The fates destroy
One a broken-down old man,
　One a boy.

One all hope, and youthful dreams,
　Life's hard journey scarce begun,
One the thorny road well trod,
　Fighting done.

Titan, Reveller in Strife,
　Couldst thou leave thy slumber deep,
At thy last descendant's fate
　Thou wouldst weep,

Knowing well how rich an ore
　May be reached if one but delves :
To what heights men under God,
　Raise themselves.

1 Judith Cowper was sister to Dr. John Cowper, Rector of Great Berkhamsted,
　　　　and therefore aunt to the poet Cowper.
2 It seems almost unnecessary to point out that the poet's name is pronounced
　　　" Cooper." He pronounced it so himself.

Youth of England, pause and weigh
  (Vice and indolence are rife),
The wondrous possibilities
  Of human life.

Think of these two. If length of years
  God gives, to use them well, decide,
If not, t'were better far that you
  A boy had died—

A victim, like the last Defoe,
  To some morose, malignant star:
A severed, than a wasted life,
  Were better far.

We lay upon his grave a flower,
  His forbear great before him aye,
He, likewise, might have made brave fight—
  We cannot say.*

But ye, your life remains. Resolve
  To strive and wait, to dare and do,
If you misuse life's precious hours
  God pardon you!

PLINY AND COWPER.

SAYS Pliny, " Oft I hunting go,
  But always, even then,
I take my well worn pocket book,
  My ink-horn and a pen.

"And while my servants place the nets
  Allow my thoughts to roam,
And thus I bring, if little game,
  My best reflections home."

So Pliny. After centuries
  A poet intersperses
A letter to a Templar friend
  With several off-hand verses.

* My writing " The Life of Daniel Defoe," brought me a good deal into connection with his descendants. I have several letters written to me by this young man.

Says he, " With gun and pencil forth
    I strolled, but the afflatus
Came first, though I was ready *in*
    Utrumque, sir, *paratus.*[1] "

Perchance the friend, to grace his shelf
    Had much preferred the rabbit,
But History e'er repeats itself
    And cannot shed the habit.

21st *October*, 1896.

GOLDSMITH AND JOHNSON AT TEMPLE BAR.

" Forsitan et nostrum nomen miscebitur istis."

ONCE Goldsmith in his plum bloom coat,
    And Johnson, stained and shabby,
At Poet's Corner chanced to meet
    Within the glorious Abbey.
Said Johnson, pointing to the busts,
    Around them, " Ah, who knows !
We may be elevated, sir;
    Ourselves, someday, with those."

No answer made his splendid friend,
    Till, having wandered far,
There came in view the grinning heads
    On gloomy Temple Bar ;
When, turning round, he slyly said,
    Whilst pointing, " Ah, who knows !
We may be elevated, sir,
    Ourselves, some day, with THOSE."

5th *Oct.* 1896.

* See the earliest preserved letter of Cowper's written to his friend " Toby."
‡ Prepared for either emergency.

EACH FOUNTAIN HATH ITS DEITY.

THE Dean for Herrick's[1] sake is dear,
Can Wordsworth lovers choose
But cherish Derwent's stream and mere !
The oft-reverting Ouse,
The limpid Avon, Bonnie Doon,"[2]
Beloved names recall,
Whilst Drayton's[3] muse confers the boon
Of poesy on all;
And thus like classic streams, you see,
Each fountain hath its deity.

TO HERRICK.

After reading his exquisite "Hesperides." Herrick died 1674.

WE love thee, Herrick, and for you
Respect thy faithful, thrifty Prue,[4]
Thy spaniel with gay ribbon pranked
To us likewise is sacrosanct.
But oh, it were a rare delight
To walk with Julia[5] home that night
When kindly glow-worms were to light her,
And slow-worms not to scare or bite her!
And just as sweet it were to go
With dainty Chloris[6] through the snow
In gemmy gown she looked so trim in.
Were never such bewitching women!
Such lips, such eyes, such pleasing tresses,
Such frim[7] and wholesome water-cresses,
Such yellow daffodils, such heavy bees,
Or verses sweet as thine Hesperides !

1 The Dean. Herrick was Vicar of Dean Prior 1629-1647. The river Dean runs through the parish.
2 Doon. Every one knows Burns's " Ye Banks and Braes o'Bonnie Doon."
3 Drayton. Michael Drayton, Author of Polyolbion, etc.
4 His housekeeper. His spaniel Tracy figures in some of the poems.
5 Mouthpiece to Julia.
6 "On Chloris walkinge in the Snowe."
7 Frim, a Buckinghamshire word—fresh and crisp.

APRIL, 1800.

AT Dereham, torn by phantoms fell
Lies tortured Cowper dying ;
At Keswick writing " Christabel "
Sits Coleridge ; and trying
His whip, Carlyle, an urchin hale
Of five, let loose from spelling
And sums, in healthy Annandale
Romps round his father's dwelling.
And so the world goes round : comes play,
Comes hey-day, comes decaying,
Alas ! each mother's son in May
Who does not do his Maying.

CRUSHING WORDSWORTH.

" AH me, that mephitic
Review ! and the critic
    With conquest is flushed.
You, Southey, well know him,
The luckless new poem
    He boasts to have crushed."

" *He*, crush 'The Excursion !'
You've some garbled version,
    Else his wits wander,
As well try to pulverize
(Give rue to purge his eyes)
    Blue Skiddaw yonder."

TO CHARLES DICKENS.

PROUD shahs with jewelled amulets and rings,
    And bangles clasping their unmanly wrists,
One must, by law, salute as King of Kings :
    Take thou the title—Prince of Humorists.
With others we have wondered, smiled, or cried,
With thee we laugh, and hold the aching side.
Allowed, thy saints—the Nells and Dombeys—bore us,
But droller devils man has yet to draw us.

Poor change were twenty Olivers for Fagin,
Or Quilp—that pigmy, pugilistic pagan ;
But when we mix with sheer, unblended motley—
Weller, Micawber ('Las their instincts bottley)—
Comes peel on peel, no mother's son resists :
Hail, Mirth-Provoker, Prince of Humorists !

25th Sept. 1896.

TO WILLIAM COWPER.

NATURE's shy hierophant,
    Oft and oft on thy career
        I have poured my lantern's glare ;
Not with motive militant,
    But to learn from cot to bier,
        All that eating Time would spare.
Others, too, have pried and gazed,
    All revere thy honoured name,
Each thy lofty motives praised,
    Hoped to live as free from blame.
None is stainless, oft indeed,
    Thou thy faults hast magnified,
Oh, that it had been thy creed,
    That for *thee* the Saviour died !

20th September, 1896.

BUNYAN'S BIRTHPLACE.

Close to Harrowden (but in Elstow Parish), near Bedford.

I WADED through the sodden field
    (Each footstep raised a clod),
To Bunyan's natal spot, but then
    The delicately shod
Should not to ploughlands make their way
Upon a damp December day.

And was it here the cottage stood,
    The brazier's forge hard by ?

Watched here the brazier's little son,
   The bright sparks upwards fly,
Whilst visions rose before his view
Of days when he would make sparks too !

One fire at least, time on, he made
   With brilliant gleams that showed
To troubled pilgrims, rich and poor,
   The Heavenly Narrow Road;
And hosts redeemed, may be, will say,
His book illumined all our way."

Some fragments of the vanished home
   Still meet the curious eye—
The broken tiles and plaster sherds
   That in the furrows lie,
But that is all, and one can best
Perceive with covered eyes the rest.

The narrow stream that flowed before
   Its step still onward sped,
With doddered willows lined ; uprose
   A teazle's bristly head ;
And right in front one still may view
The elmy, sloping avenue.

A stone's throw off a farmstead looms
   With dovehouse, barn, and sty,
I turned to go, but in such plight
   I felt nigh forced to cry—
While sinking in the treacherous slough—
With Pliable, "Where are you now ?"

But, like him, too, I scrambled out,
   And live my tale to tell :
The road beyond is half a lake,
   I raised a mussel shell—
A relic still I'm rather fond
Of showing from the Slough Despond.

Adieu, wet Pesselynton field !
   Much, John, as I revere
Thy memory I would not pitch
   My tabernacle here—
A dryer spot, more snugly placed,
Were more to my peculiar taste.

     28th December, 1896.

THE PALACE BEAUTIFUL.

It is not unlikely that Hillersden Manor House, close to Elstow Church was the original of the Palace Beautiful in "The Pilgrim's Progress." One notices with interest the large scallop shell—the pilgrim's emblem— cut boldly in the wood the door.

THIS ruin with its ivied walls
The "Palace Beautiful" recalls,
　　We see beside its door
And scupltured porch the pilgrim stand,
His staff and precious roll in hand—
　　Afar the lions roar.

We hear the clear toned porter's bell,
And see the serious damosell
　　Unto whose lashes came
Bright drops when Christian told his tale
Of check and fright by hill and dale—
　　His mission, and his name.

And still upon the door we view
The scallop shell that pilgrims true,
　　To sacred altars wore.
But Prudence now, and Piety,
And supra-lovely[1] Charity
　　Attend us at the door

With welcomes; when they catechise,
With what poor wit within us lies
　　We answer.　Then they showed
The armoury where breastplates hung,
The sling and stones that David slung,
　　And Shamgar's famous goad.

Small task it were to recognise
The chamber " Peace,"[2] for saffron skies
　　And sun at dawn one sees,
Again explory we resume,
And in the munimental room
　　Inspect old pedigrees.

Like Christian then upon the leads
We mount—the glorious campaign spreads
　　Before our wondering eye ;
In fancy only, for to-day
Its passages and rooms display
　　No cover but the sky.

1 I. Cor. XIII., 13.
2 "Whose windows opened towards the sun-rising."

They harness us from head to heel,
Give sword of tested Milan steel,
  Some raisins, wine and bread ;
And forth we go, equipped to meet
Apollyon huge, with ursine feet,
  Red dart, and scaly head.

Surrendered now, this stately house,
To owlet, sparrow, bat, and mouse,
  But on this portico—
These mullioned windows, wide, unglazed—
We like to think the pilgrim gazed
  Two centuries ago.

                              3rd. January, 1897

ELSTOW GREEN.

A CHURCH, with tower apart, that peeps between
Its elms ; a hall[1] that stood when Kate was queen
  And Harry king ; an ancient shaft of stone
With pedestal—'tis peaceful Elstow Green.

To yonder belfry oft as eve recurred
Flew Bunyan, blither than a singing bird,
  To ring the bells.   His gentle wife at home[2]
Could hear them, and their poor blind Mary heard.

When on the Green were baited bull or bear,
And booths and stalls stood round about—to share
  The song and dance he ran : I think we've been
To Vanity and seen its famous Fair.

On Sundays to this sward full oft he bore
His sharpened tip-cat, played, and cursed, and swore ;
  And here he heard the holy, heavenly voice
That made him pause, and bade him sin no more.

Lo, one tremendous theme absorbs his brain,
He stops his ears—the voice resounds again—
  " Eternity ! Am I prepared ! " he cries ;
So sticks the horseleech to the burning vein.

1 The Moot Hall.
2 Bunyan's Cottage, which he inhabited from 1649 to 1655, and in which his
blind child Mary was born (1650), is still shown though it has been much altered.
The " wife," his first wife, who died in 1658.
For a fourth poem dealing with Bunyan, " Bunyan's Christmas " see p. 81.

May we, too, hear that message—you and I—
And, musing here, and on this theme, apply
The moral to our precious souls likewise :
We, too, who throb with life, must some day die.

4th January, 1896.

EDWARD FITZGERALD AT BEDFORD.

(Of Omar Khayyám fame).

Edward FitzGerald, born 1809, died 1883.

WHENE'ER, with can and rods, I see
A pair of anglers cross the lea
I think, rare Edward Fitz,[1] of thee,
    And piscatorial Browne ;[2]
The willows you so loved still blow,
Your poplars stand in solemn row—
Such shafts as only Ouse can show
    By pleasant Bedford town.

About each lane and river nook,
You "poked with colour-box and book,"
And oft your way together took
    From Bedford unto Bletsoe.
You pause before "The Angler's Rest ;"
Methinks the cup was in request
With Omar—Has he not confessed !—
    A custom I regret so.

We see you in Piscator's close
Lie sunning, pleased, desidiose,[3]
Your boots—while Omar's lines engross—
    Bright yellow dust all over ;
The filly, snuffing round you, worse
Than mad conceives you ; she prefers
To books of dainty Persian verse
    Rich buttercups and clover.

1 Thackeray, Tennyson and Carlyle, called FitzGerald affectionately "Old Fitz."

2 Alderman William Browne of Bedford, "Piscator," FitzGerald's host and friend. He died from a dreadful accident in 1859.

3 Desidiose, an old fashioned word—lazy,

On Sunday morn your stick you reach
And haste to hear bold Matthews preach,
In way that "shakes your soul," while each
    And every round are sobbing;
And when at night in bed you lie,
Old Samuel Johnson's bookcase by,
And looking-glass, in vain you try
    To sleep—the heart still throbbing.

But by-and-by we miss you here,
No longer over Bedfordshire
You "potter." Lo, Piscator's bier!
    Friend after friend disperses.
Your preacher too! Your heartstrings ache,
You follow in his coffin's wake.[1]
We love all anglers for your sake,
    Accept, dear ghost, these verses.

5th January, 1897.

---

[1] Rev. T. R. Matthews (died 4th September, 1845). A stirring Bedford evangelist.

SUBJECTS FROM ANCIENT HISTORY.

THE ARTIFICE OF KING AMASIS.

A story from Herodotus.

To EGYPT's king, Cambyses penned
    A note : " My hopes excite me,
I love your daughter, kindly send
    The girl, and you'll delight me."

Amasis, caring not to wed,
    Just then, his only daughter,
Bedecked another girl instead
    With stones of finest water ;

And into Persia as his own
    Despatched her.   She was fêted,
And king Cambyses on his throne
    Himself congratulated.

He praised her lips, her faultless nose,
    Her ankles—which between us,
Were not a whit less neat than those
    Ascribed by bards to Venus.

At last the secret outward got,
    And on mature reflection
He found her eyes and lips were not—-
    Her nose was not—perfection.

And in his wrath an armed horde
    He raised.   Its forces serried
He led, to try the power of sword,
    Nor knew that, dead and buried,

His foe had checked him.   So the gods
    Decreed.   Exasperated,
The wretched corpse he beat with rods
    And what was left cremated.

And so if any swain apply
    Politely for your daughter
Say " yes " or " no," but do not try
    To cheat an honest courter.

To palm on simple gentlemen
  The wrong girl, a disgrace is,
And history might repeat again
  The sentence of Amasis.

23rd. September, 1896.

THE ABSURD CONDUCT OF HIPPOCLIDES.

A story from Herodotus.

Of all the tales of courting
  The funniest to us
Appears the one embedded
  In old Herodotus.

King Clisthenes,[1] a daughter
  Accomplished had, and sweet,
And those who hoped to court her
  Were in his hall to meet.

Came epicures and sages
  To pay their warm addresses,
And princes ; in the market
  Not always are princesses.

Advantage o'er the others
  Was soon attained by one,
Hippoclides[2] of Athens,
  Tisander's handsome son.

But trembled soon his chances,
  For when amid the babel
The fiddlers played a merry tune
  He leaped upon the table.

And with self-satisfaction,
  Of all men seen, he prances,
The Athens dance first executes,
  And then the Spartan dances.

Nor sees the monarch biting,
  His lip until it bled,
And finished up his antics
  By standing on his head.

1 Clisthenes. Three syllables, accent on first.
2 Hippoclides. Four syllables, accent on second.

" Your very fine achievements
  I wish not to disparage,
But," said the king, " Sir Acrobat,
  You've danced away your marriage."

But some with equanimity
  Can disappointment bear,
Our lover could, " Hippoclides,"
  He answered, " does not care."

And so right down the ages
  The saying passed ; whene'er
A Greek is balked, " Hippoclides,"
  He comments, " does not care."

And England with fair Sicyon
  The time-old saying shares,
We don't bring in Hippoclides,
  But we often say—" Who cares ? "

14th September, 1896.

PYTHIUS'S MILLIONS.

A story from Herodotus.

WHEN Xerxes led a continent
  To Greece, impelled by spleen, he
Upon his way used up a day
  At Phrygian Celænae,

Where Pythius, its wealthy son,
  The mighty king attended,
And set before the multitude
  An entertainment splendid.

No bagatelle it is to serve
  A citadel with rations,
What was it then to feed a king
  And half a dozen nations !

The dinner done, about his host
  The king would know, and who
He was. " The richest man on earth,
  My lord, excepting you."

To Pythius then. " Thy purse they say,
  Is longer than Meander,[1]
What are you worth ? "—" My noble guest,
  I'll answer you with candour.

1 A river of Asia Minor.

" Of millions I have nearly four
    In staters, lands beside,
If you'll accept the cash I'm sure
    You'll leave me gratified."

" My Lydian friend, I dearly love
    True friends, and now I've found one,
How many thousands do you need
    To make the sum a round one ? "

"Exactly seven."   Then turned the king
    To his administraters,
And bade them hand to Pythius
    The odd seven thousand staters.

" Your millions four are now complete,"
    Observed the King. " I'm willing—
I'm proud— to be your friend, but I
    Decline to take a shilling."

Now some with this old Persian tale
    Do very justly quarrel,
As in it, for the life of them,
    They cannot see a moral.

But some fine day, to make it up,
    I'll win me further glory
And write a moral just as long
    Without a grain of story.

IT'S VERY SAD.

THEY tell me that Herodotus
    Is slippery and mendacious,
That fibbing Marco Polo seems
    Beside him quite veracious.

Now this is sad, but what is worse,
    I cannot snap my fetter,
For when I try to love him less
    I only love him better.

                                11th October, 1896.

OMPHALE.

You know the myth of Omphale
   The famous Lydian queen,
And how big-chested Hercules
   Was sold to service mean.
Ah me, why did Fate
Bring him to that parlous state!

She stole his lion's skin, and gave
   A woman's gown instead,
She popped a distaff in his hand,
   Poked hairpins in his head;

And then because he spun so ill
   In tea-cup storm she flew,
And at his rough Titanic head
   Her pretty sandal threw.

She rouged his cheeks, with henna dyed
   His elephantine feet,
In fine, his transformation brought
   To woman most complete.

Just then, a little shaft discharged
   Attained its mark so well
That from a spit-fire she became
   A gentle-eyed gazelle.

She gave him back his knobby club,
   His lion's skin likewise,
She washed the henna from his feet,
   The stibium from his eyes.*

The distaff she had made him use
   Upon the fire she threw,
The slipper that had bruised his head
   She promptly tore in two.

Flew all the carmine from her cheek,
   The sparkles from her eye,
Instead of imprecative threat
   Escaped the long-drawn sigh.

The food she ate would scarcely feed
   A sparrow or a mouse,
"The pile prepare, I soon must quit,"
   Said she, " this earthly house."

* Eastern ladies stain their feet yellow with henna, and their eyelids black with stibium.

" Oh, lady dear," said Hercules,
  " What can—what shall we do !
The world were not a world at all
  Without a glimpse of you."

Again her eyes grew bright, again
  Each cheek became a peach,
And round his neck she flung her arms
  As far as they could reach.

The cheeks that she was wont to slap
  She covered up with kisses,
No more she beat his mountain back,
  Said he, " Most wondrous this is ! "

" I am not what I was, my love,
  . I thought, dear love, "said she,
" To metamorphose you, but you
  Have metamorphosed me."

THE VOICE OF ALARIC.

ERE Alaric his heathens
  Led southerly to try
Conclusions with the Romans
  He called his captains nigh,

And unto them, '' My comrades,
  Scarred, shaggy, wiry, brave,
I seek," said he," in Italy
  A kingdom or a grave."

Shall we from his bold purpose
  Take profit, you and I ?
Clear comes from Busentinus [1]
  The forceful conqueror's cry :

" Up, up, ye puny weaklings,
  Who rust in sloth at home,
And like the ancient heathen,
  Hew out your way to Rome ;

" And I will promise bullion,
  And if you avid are
For pepper, tons of pepper
  From spicy Malabar." [2]

12th Sept., 1896.

1 The river in whose bed Alaric was buried.

2 Alaric consented to raise the siege of Rome on the payment of 5,000 pounds of gold, 30,000 pounds of silver, and 3,000 pounds weight of pepper.

IT WAS SOCRATES.

Countryman:

" In Athens yesternight I met
The oddest creature I had set
    My eyes upon for weeks,
Lo, two projecting eyes, but those
Were tempered by a turned-up nose,
    That sank between his cheeks.

" His bulk was vast, his feet were bare,
To see him stride about and stare
    At every passer near,
Unnerved me so, I thought in him
A satyr from the woodlands dim
    I saw, with pipes and leer.

" And sometimes in an absent fit,
He'd face a spot, and stare at it,
    Like statue made of stone.
A scarecrow oft is better clad,
Grotesque his air, his language had
    A rough and caustic tone.

" And very superciliously,
The clumsy monster gazed on me."

Athenian:

" The portrait, knave, agrees
Precisely with his look and mien;
Barbarian, thou hast heard and seen
Immortal Socrates."

3rd Nov. 1896.

ALCIBIADES AND THE SCHOOLMASTER.

A story from Plutarch.

' Tis said that Alcibiades[1]
(The tale hath an aroma
Unique) once craved, a friend to please,
The Odyssey of Homer;

1 Alcibiades, five syllables, accent on third.

And so into a school-house nigh
  He dropped, and straightway stated
His need.   The pedagogue's reply
  His calling poorly mated.

Said he, " The volume I have not.
  Of him I've nought I fear."
Quoth Alcibiades, " Great Scott ! "
  And boxed the master's ear.

To act like that is not polite
  In hamlet, town, or city.   Him,
However, it served nearly right,
  At least we don't much pity him.

THE DEMI-GOD.

Suggested by reading Plutarch's " Alexander the Great."

WHEN a demi-god by day
  Chances devious to stray
Straight away before him goes
In the sky a flock of crows,
Keeping, too, their favourite right
With their croaking in the night.

When the prophets prophesy
That which savours of a lie,
And in which beholders see
Sheer impossibility,
Demi-gods, like me or you,
Do the deed, and make it true.

"THOU WOMAN'S PROPERTY."

Dryden's Virgil.

The supposed address of Hermes to Æneas enslaved by Dido.

TROJAN, did almighty Jove
Send thee here to loll in love ?
Is thy highest destiny
But a woman's slave to be !
Scented, broidered, gemmed, belaced,
With her scarf about thy waist.
Who would such a poppet be !
Faugh ! thou woman's property.

Thou of Troja once the pride,
True a sword adorns thy side,
Nay, a toy with gems besprent,
Not for use but ornament.
Couches soft, in silks arrayed,
Jove ! for this were muscles made !
Gather round, high gods, and see.
Faugh ! thou woman's property.

Here in shame Æneas lies,
Still unslain his enemies,
Of the city he should found
Not a stone hath touched the ground,
Even his own captains sneer,
Mutter almost in his ear,
" This ! can this our leader be,
This—a woman's property ! "

Trojan, rouse, throw off the net,
Fling away thy baubles, whet
Once again thy tarnished sword,
Doff the slave, and don the lord,
Rise while yet 'tis called to-day,
Fling, oh fling these toys away,
Anything you will be, be
Save a woman's property.

Stung with these eating taunts, and touched his pride,
Æneas rose, the trinket at his side
He snapped in twain, the gemmy scarf he tore,
And, braced in iron, sought the sounding shore,
His soldiers marked him, and a great cheer rent
Like winds uproarious all the firmament—
Oh, sweet it is from sloth to be set free
To who hath been but woman's property !

34

LUCIUS DOMITIUS.

The story of Lucius Domitius is briefly as follows :—When Julius Cæsar marched
southward to oppose Pompey every city submitted except Corfinium, held by L.
Domitius Ahenobarbus. But Cæsar had no sooner invested it than the garrison
betrayed their commander, and delivered him up to the enemy. Fearing the
resentment of the conqueror, Domitius ordered one of his slaves to bring a cup of
poison, and he drank. Cæsar, however, to show his moderation in the midst of
victory, granted to his captive life and liberty. Domitius now regretted his rash
act, but at this moment the slave sprang forward with the assurance that the
potion had not been poison at all, but only a sleeping draught. As reward the
slave was manumitted.

SPEAKING pictures never tire ;
Here's a story old and trite—
Toddling child and tottering sire
　　Know it—'tis a sunstreak bright
　　Crossing Cæsar's history.

He from Gaul in fury brought
All his eagles, all his powers ;
Humbly every stronghold sought
　　Friendship save the stubborn towers
　　Girding swart Corfinium.

Closed the ponderous gates abide,
　" Courage ! every faithful man,
Stem we first this baleful tide,
　　Die we then as Romans can,"
　　Quoth Lucius Domitius.

" Arrow, bolt, and bar, thy track
Shall restrain at least a day,
Back to Gaul, vile traitor, back—
　　Jove ! Eheu ! Do friends betray
　　Lucius Domitius !

" Chains for slaves, and slavery !
Thee, High Thunderer, I thank,
Fitter meed awaiteth me,"
　　As the poison cup he drank,
　　Lucius uttered haughtily.

Now in Cæsar's camp conveyed,
　　Careless what his foe may say,
Well he knows the poison's raid
　　Soon will end the hated day,
　　Soon will baffle tyranny.

Fair were Cæsar's words though few,
" Thou hast been a haughty foe,
Would thou wert a friend and true !
Roman, unmolested go."
Silent stood Domitius.

Truly conquered now, he bends,
" This from him my soul did hate !
Generous foe, perfidious friends !
Cæsar come thy words too late,
Poison inly scorches me."

" Master, master," cries a slave,
Look, my noble master, up,
" Harmless was the draught I gave,
Innocent the hemlock cup,
Filled with wine the purest."

This old story like a star
Lighting history's pages shows
That the meanest sometimes are
Strong to aid—that bitterest foes
May command our benison.

MY ANGRY GODS, OR PLEASE SPARE MY BOOKS AND PICTURES.

Fabius Maximus, who had no taste for the arts, having taken Tarentum, it was asked him what was to be done with its masterpieces of painting and sculpture. To which he replied, "Let us leave to the Tarentines their angry gods," in allusion to the attitudes in which the gods of Tarentum were generally represented.

WHEN Fabius to pillage
Tarentum gave, and sent
Each citizen to tillage,
The mines, or banishment,

" We've stripped them of their fleeces,
But how," enquired his men,
" About the masterpieces
Of chisel, brush and pen ?"

But eye artistic lacking,
Said he, " Care I for clods ?
Or daubs ? As not worth packing,
We'll leave their " ANGRY GODS "

I like the answer scabious
Of this blunt dog of war,
And, imitating Fabius,
Should robber force my door

With fancy for my purse, he
Might pardon gain, 'tis odds,
By leaving in his mercy
My precious "ANGRY GODS."

ON A NOBLE RECENTLY-PURCHASED COPY OF HOBBES'S THUCYDIDES.

O NOBLE volume with luxurious text,
And ample notes, long s's, u's for v's ;
Whilst terminating each brave page one sees
(Archaic rule) the word that starts the next.
A gallery complete, the frontispiece ;
Lo, Athens, Sparta, noble Pericles,
King Archidamus—and Thucydides
His learned self—a tree-filled map of Greece.
A demagogue is some rapt crowd addressing,
An army marches, and a navy floats.
Who are those spearmen ? Who propel those boats?
Like child an orange ripe and large caressing,
I long to taste, yet tease myself.   Arise
The waters to my mouth.   I pat my prize.

20th September, 1896.

PRAXINOE IN TROUBLE.

Suggested by the 15th Idyll of Theocritus.

I SENT my spouse to buy ceruse
And nitre from the stall,
But what he brought's of little use,
If any good at all.

There is not—really I could cry—
A pinch upon my shelf,
I feared they'd cheat a man, but I
Could not go out myself.

I'm sure this evening at the show
　Although there's no comparing
Her eyes with mine, at someone else
　The folk will all be staring.

But if this e'er occur again
　It's very odd to me,
The things in common use 'tis wise
　To have in quantity.

My sky at last has lost its speck,
　I'm happier now and brighter,
Of best ceruse I'll have a peck,
　And half a peck of nitre.*

* Ceruse (white lead), and nitre were much used by Roman ladies in their toilettes

POEMS RELATING TO OLNEY, AND VICINITY.

BORN IN OLNEY.

The Author felicitates himself and all others who drew their first breath in the town.

The first requisite of happiness is, that a man be born in a famous town.—*Euripides.*

WHATEVER path before us lies,
    Let fortune smile or frown,
It's very clear that we were born
    Within a famous town.

And what, forsooth, were you and I
    That we were favoured thus!
That Fate so many other folk
    Should pass, to smile on us!

But that we lived before this life
    The ancients all agree—
"The Pre-existence" (Useful creed!)
    "Of Souls;" so possibly

When in that state we did some deeds
    Deserving of applause,
And though I have forgotten mine
    You may remember yours.

Our looks and purse may go, but Time
    Can not, howe'er he frown,
Abduct the fact that we were born
    Within a famous town.

6th October, 1896.

NEWTON IN THE PLANTANES.

John Newton was for several years a slave on one of the Plantanes, a group of islands off Sierra Leone, where he was cruelly treated by his master's wife, a black woman named Pee-Eye.

WHEN Olney's bold Apostle,
In raging fever lay
Within his Plantane island,
On couch of filthy hay;
His life at Pee-Eye's mercy,
Suspended by a thread,
Begrudged a drop of water,
A wretched crust of bread,

Would you have dared to augur,
That this vile wretch who raves,
Profane among profaners,
A servant unto slaves,
Would ever scale mount Zion?
That Heaven his sins would blot?
But God can "loose Orion,"[1]
And mortals "know Him not."[2]

20th September, 1896.

WESTON PARK.

In reference to the following lines, Mr. Alfred Austin, the Poet Laureate, in a letter to the author (4th October 1896), says:—I have always had a very tender feeling for Cowper............But the man himself and the ministers of grace who abetted his genius, softened his sorrows, and refined his home, are more interesting even than his poems. You are fortunate in dwelling in a spot sanctified by the recollection of the poet's pious breath.

AH, Weston Park, how speak of thee
With calmness! Words discover
The hidden springs. So throbs the pulse
When lover lisps of lover.

Thy groves delight, be vaulted sky
Cerulean or sober,
But, Oh, their fragrance when thy leaves
Lie knee-deep in October!

1 Job. XXVIII., 31. Idea, a great rebel bound in the sky.
2 Job. XXXVI., 26. God is great, and we know him not.

This springy sod Throckmortons trod,
    In classic prose and ballad
Immortalised—Sir Nicholas
    Who ate the poisoned salad;

Sir Robert's dame, whose graven tomb
    Was wrecked by goths destructive;
Sir John, Sir John's distinguished guest
    Who sang its charms seductive,

For here, a hat his escritoire,
    " Sir Cowper" verse composes,
Here Catherina mushrooms plucks,
    And gives her cheeks new roses.

Here saunters lovely " Mrs. Frog,"[1]
    And lovelier Lady Austen,
And Cowper's Mary, Beau, the dog,
    This bosky maze gets lost in.

Here Newton rhymed, came earnest Scott[2]
    With bible late and early,
Its fame allured Hugh Miller spare
    Elihu Burritt burly.

Their airy shades still haunt these glades:
    Could buoyant bard or sober
Inhale unmoved the labdanum
    Of Weston in October!

A SINGULAR PERSON.

When John Newton was at St. Kitts in the West Indies, he was looked upon as very singular because he used to say his prayers. When he asked the people whether he was the only singular person they had met with, they said they remembered one other, a planter, but he had been dead several years.

St. Kitts is in a flutter
    And every-body stares,
For, oddly, in the ship at port
    The captain says his prayers.

Mulattoes flock, and Saxons,
    And negroes black as pitch,
And hardly more sensation
    Could griffin cause or witch.

1 Cowper's playful name for Mrs. (afterwards Lady) Throckmorton,
2 The Commentator,

" Has e'er another oddity
Amazed your eyes and ears ? "
Said Newton. "We remember one
But he's been dead for years."

" Like you he never missed a day,
And prayed in just your style
But, since, we do not think there's been
Another in the isle,

So if we seem demented,
And run agape to gaze,
You must not mind, it seems so odd
To see a man who prays."

29th Oct. 1896.

COWPER'S POPLAR FIELD.

To the Rev. G. Wilson, M.A., Aug. 1895.

The field was probably Lynch Close, near Lavendon Mill, but it is not known
where the poplars stood.

WE sought the poet's poplar field,
Beside the ancient, rumbling mill,
Tall poplars still around it yield
Cool shadow ; Ouse reflects them still.

We heard the waters' angry note,
The bark of dog, the hum of bee,
We saw the bridge, the chain-moored boat,
Green island, osier tree,

The " preaching barn " that crowns the crest
Recalling Bull, good, portly man,
And Newton, by his audience blessed,
But not by his diocesan.[1]

We pried within the low-ceiled mill.
Lo, mighty beams of darkened oak,
The slow-revolving, groaning wheel,
With dripping nave and spoke !

[1] The bishop objected to Newton preaching outside his own parish.

But where the trees in Cowper's day
    Low whispered, no man knows,
At most, the curious can but weigh
    Vexatious con's and pro's.

Perplexity rewards our pains,
    We are but mocked, the thing is hid,
And Time, whose ancient chest contains
    The clew, declines to raise the lid.

O bargainer for carven oak,
    And battered curios without name,
If ever by some happy stroke,
    You see that chest, secure the same.

No matter where, in street or court,
    In church or chapel, boat or barge,
Or tavern, if it can be bought
    Secure it, never mind the charge,

And then the lock, with breathless haste,
    We'll force, and baffled Time shall yield
(What though in triple iron cased)
    The secret of the Poplar Field.

DR. JOHNSON AT EASTON MAUDIT.

(Near Olney).

A SUMMER once great Johnson spent
    (Old Fleet Street's darling son)
At Easton—exiled twenty weeks
    From tavern, post, and dun.

Beneath this row of filbert trees
    Each morn his walk he took,
His elephantine form he flung
    Each evening in this nook.

Here listened he to Percy's song,
    "Oh, Nanny," praised the piece,
And when 'twas over sought the pond
    And fed her ducks and geese.

And bluntly said, she had more sense
    Than had her spouse the vicar,
You still may see the pond, may taste
    The Doctor's favourite liquor

In Percy's parlour.   Yonder church
   The snorting sage attended,
The dropping banners still are there,
   The tombs of sculpture splendid.

How Johnson passed those twenty weeks
   With nobody to listen—
The man who " talked for victory "—
   Where once a year they christen,

Where none or hardly any wed,
   And burials are as rare
As bustards, where save note of lark
   No sound salutes the air,

With no-one but the vicar's wife,
   The vicar's cow, and tup
And several pigs—we could not say
   So, baffled, give it up.

No doubt 'twas with intense relief
   The coach he reascended,
And turned to London's darling din,
   His trying furlough ended,

Himself condoling—had he missed
   The penance and the pain,
The pleasure he had lost likewise
   Of going back again.

                    5th Oct., 1896.

WRITTEN IN BOW BRICKHILL CHURCHYARD.

I UP here on hillocks lie,
   Viewing hade, and copse, and town,
So upon Olympus high
   Omni-powerful Jove looked down.

Once to see the pains men took
   But to gain some giddy height
Staggered me.   Around I look
   All the wonderment takes flight.

In part, perhaps, because I view
   The vastly panoramic show ;
The paly line of distant blue,
   The floating, fleecy clouds like snow,

And all the chequered valley blent
  With bistre, yellow, vert, and vair;
But, too, because its evident
  That I'm up here and you're down there.

28th July, 1896.

A CHRISTMAS GREETING.

Written on a Christmas Card.

A CHRISTMAS Greeting, piping hot,
From Olney, Bucks, the favoured spot
Where Cowper wrote, and Newton led
His flock to Christ the Fountain Head.

May Cowper's humour light your hearth, ·
  And Newton's fervour steep you,
The God of both direct your path,
  And ever bless and keep you.

Xmas, 1896.

THE BOOKSTALL IN THE DERNGATE.

A LOADSTONE in Northampton stands,
  So difficult to go by,
That e'en the siren rocks of old
  Were easier much to row by.

It's hollowed out—above are books,
  Whichever way you turn pate
Its books, and books, and books—You know
  The Bookstall in the Derngate.

Unto that Temple of the Nine
  I owe the tome I tried for
So long, the tall Thucydides
  That half my friends have sighed for.

I got him too for half a song—
  A modest outlay surely—
Most precious is Herodotus,
  I value Lord Macaulay—

But as for that delightful set,
  My aromatic Gibbon,
Not dearer to a mother's heart
  Is baby with a bib on.

They all from that same cavern came.
Should cyclone over-turn gate,
Wreck street, and square—'twill surely spare
The Bookstall in the Derngate.

If e'er the Germans come, and shell
Church, chimney, jail; and burn gate
'Tis clear the town would flock to save
The Bookstall in the Derngate.

And if the earth should all collapse,
(A very sad and stern fate),
One pile, I trust, will still be left—
The Bookstall in the Derngate.

27th Sept., 1896.

AT THE SUMMER-HOUSE.

An imaginary tête-à-tête.

WE sat within the Summer-house,
Said I, "Dear bard and friend,
It seems to me, this tenement
Is slightly on the bend.

" By all means, if you're so inclined,
Within its walls abide,
But, if you've no objection, I
Would rather sit outside."

But by and by a shower came on
When, almost without thinking,
I popped within by Cowper's side
For shelter in a winking.

Said Cowper, "Dear Biographer,"
As chirruping we sat,
Although you're chary of your skin
You're charier of your hat."

Said I, "Good sir, a ruined hat
No ointment can restore,
But broken skins may heal, and e'en
Get sounder than before."

Then on his face there spread a cloud
    " And is that so ? " said he,
" Would God a wounded soul could heal
    Its rent as easily ! "

And then we both in silence sat
    Within the fragile cell,
The whiles, without, great painful drops
    Upon the rose-leaves fell.

Although a trifle—scarcely worth
    A drop of ink may-be—
This little incident reflects
    His life's epitome.

WHEN OLNEY'S UNDER SNOW.

THE days are short, the winds are keen,
    The streams have ceased to flow,
The robins from our fingers feed—
    And Olney's under snow.

The chubby boys with crimson cheeks
    Well-kneaded snowballs throw,
Which now and then a window take—
    When Olney's under snow.

Lo, youth and beauty, skates in hand,
    Towards the meadows go ;
For pairing there is much excuse
    When Olney's under snow.

And if without there's spurge and yew
    Within there's mistletoe—
A plant the parish much affects
    When Olney's under snow.

The sermons of the blithe New Year—[1]
    A triple series—show
That One above is in our thoughts
    When Olney's under snow.

Spares Charity her coals and clothes—
    Good deeds like diamonds glow—
And queues of men and barrows form
    When Olney's under snow.

[1] The " New Year's sermon " on the first three days of every year have been preached without intermission, at the three places of worship, ever since the days of John Newton.

All hail, ye pious souls[2] to whom
  The poor these favours owe,
We think of you not once or twice
  When Olney's under snow.

The tempests bellow through the woods
  Like bull or buffalo,
The steeple and the poplars swing
  When Olney's under snow.

To avalanche and glacial sights
  Let those who laud them go ;
The sight is good enough for me
  Of Olney under snow.

2 Richard Pierson (died 1626), and other founders of the Feoffee Charity which distributes coal; and Ann Hopkins Smith who built the Almshouses, and left forty pounds a year to buy clothing for the poor.

MISCELLANEOUS POEMS.

WHEN JESUS DWELT IN JEWRY.

WHEN Jesus dwelt in Jewry
　　Whate'er he did or said
　　He drew upon his head
The Pharisaic fury,
It is the whole world's way
　　If any wrong oppose
He must encounter every day
　　A host of spiteful foes.

And if our sinless Master
　　Did daily suffer pain
Shall we amid disaster
　　And obloquy complain ?
I tremble for thy fate
　　If none desire thy fall,
　　And thou art praised by all,
And none despise or hate.

It's weigh, and work, and force,
　　And act, and do, and go,
It's madness to avoid a course
　　Because you dread a foe ;
In every path and way
　　Who seeks the " Golden Fleece,"
　　Like Tyro's son of Greece,[1]
Must first the dragon slay.

Your duty 'tis to work
　　And use your treasure hoard,
The men who duty shirk
　　Will have to face their Lord ;
You well the day may dread
　　That shall proclaim thy dearth
Of all except that slugabed
　　Poor talent in the earth.

[1] Jason, son of Tyro, sailed to Colchis and carried off the Golden Fleece.

If aught could add a terror
To whoso death surveys,
It is the fatal error
Of having lost his days—
The days that wasted flee;
Pray God they be but few,
And that small blame ensue
For them on you and me !

KINGS NEVER DROWN.

At the news of a rebellion at Le Mans, William Rufus flung himself into the first boat he could find, and crossed the Channel in the face of a storm. "Kings never drown," he replied contemptuously to the remonstrances of his followers.

NONE and nothing harm can do
If you're bold and brave,
Something may be learnt by you
From a heartless knave.

Crossing to the Norman shore
In the tempest's whirl,
William's courtiers trembling more
Than a timid girl,

Wished they were (Heroic choice !)
Safe in Plymouth town.
" Cowards ! " cried a scornful voice,
" Kings never drown."

Face the glass—whate'er your lot—
O'er the mantel shelf
Do you see a king ?   If not,
Promptly crown yourself.

Pour the unguent courage, pray,
Tightly grip your crown,
Make for any shore and say,
"Kings never drown ! "

LET ME BE ALONE.

On hearing that she had become Queen, our Sovereign, turning to the Duchess of Kent, said, ' Let me be alone, dear mother—for a long time.'

WHEN to our lady, on this glorious throne,
First came the news that she must reign, a throng
Of thoughts distraught. ' Let me be quite alone,'
She said, ' my dearest mother, and for long.'
She had her wish. The feeble and the strong
In crucial times have need of solitude.
What of the future ? Though with strength endued,
Empires have sunk. 'Tis easy to go wrong,
But one great Master ever holds the keys
Of life and death. They found her on her knees.
Pathetic story. What can England fear,
If but her people righteousness revere,
Defend the weak, thwart tyrants, just abide,
Lean hard on God, and take His ' Book ' for guide ! *

THE BEAUTIFUL CUFAN.

OF Plinys and Calphurnias
'Tis very hard to tire,
An Arab loved his Cufan bride
As little boys love fire,
And from his ravishing and peerless prize
He scarcely ever could remove his eyes.

But on a melancholy day
The cadi chanced to see her,
And from the youth he snatched away
His little, dainty dear;
As all remonstrance stood for nought
The case was to the caliph brought,

Who bade the cadi straight return
The girl. " My lord, as she
Is so delicious, let her stay
A little while with me,
For just one year—one year,"—he said,
" Then, if you like, strike off my head."

* For this poem the author received a letter of thanks from Her Majesty the Queen, 19th October, 1896.

The words astonished. Said the prince,
  " Go bring the girl." They brought her,
" I do not wonder at their taste,
  I'd like you, too, dear daughter,"
Said he, " I've fifty wives, all youthsome,
But none—there is not one so toothsome.

" You tempt indeed, but justice e'er
  Has marked our noble line,
Decide yourself, my girl, will you
  Be his, or his, or mine ? "
" I'm not deserving of more honour, clearly,"
She said, " and, sire, I love my husband dearly."

" Bravo ! then go, enamoured pair ;
  May nothing disenchant !—
And, cadi, if your heart is sore,
  Hath mine no irritant !
But justice, as you clearly know,
Is justice, therefore, cadi, go."

                              11th October, 1896.

BALSAC'S PENNY.

Poor, slaving Balzac, with his fate
  Excusably would bicker ;
Toil as he would, his creditors
  More clamorous grew and thicker ;

And if a nimble franc arrived
  He'd scarcely blessed the senders
Ere gaped like chasms bottomless
  The mouths of money-lenders.

At last he cried, " If e'er I have,
  With nobody to claim it,
A penny of my very own,
  I'll mount, and glaze, and frame it."

BALSAC AND THE THIEF.

One night as Balzac lay in bed
  He thought he heard a rumbling ;
And, looking up, about his desk
  Observed a burglar fumbling.

Whereat into a loud guffaw
   He burst. Quite disconcerted,
"Whatever are you laughing at?"
   The baffled rascal blurted.

" I laugh because such pains you take
   By night,—though night's your haytime—
To rummage where the owner ne'er
   Could find a sou by daytime."

                 19th September, 1896.

"WHEN A GOD DESIRES TO RIDE."

When a god wishes to ride, any chip or pebble will bud, and shoot out winged feet, and serve him for a horse.—Emerson.

WHEN a god desires to ride
   Any chip or straw will do,
Winglets sprout on either side—
   Glows the deity in you?
Grip the nearest, handiest bough,
   Bury spur, like arrow go,
Ride for dearest life, and thou
   Hell itself shalt overthrow.

                 24th September, 1896.

BELIEF IN ONE'S-SELF.

IF you would anything achieve
   Take care no doubts conceive in you,
For in yourself you must believe
   To make the world believe in you.

ERASMUS'S ADVICE.

WORK hard,
   Look at me,
   Regular be
      At labour;
Disregard
   The opinion
   Of minion
      And neighbour;

Like Cato,
Study Plato ;
Short is life
  And miry,
Love your wife,
  Keep a diary.

9th November, 1896.

BY TRYING.

By trying, got the Greeks in Troy,
  And Taric conquered Spain,
By trying, plodding Ferdinand
  Obtained it back again.

By trying you can traverse sea,
  Lagoon, morass, or dyke,
And as a rule can get to be
  Precisely what you like.

THE TEACHING OF EPICTETUS.

Phrygia's fine philosopher
  Taught that things respecting man
Into two divisions fall   .
  (He adored by Arrian) :
First the things within our pale ;
  Thoughts, aversions, deeds, and all
Aspirations and desires
  Justly we our own may call.
Next the things that senseless man
  Looks upon as boon or bane :
Honour, greatness, health and wealth
  Own no lord or suzerain :
Lack of these, or loss, should stir
No devout philosopher.

FOOTBALL AT CALAIS

At Calais once some English who
  Among their traps had put ball,
For lack of other sport, arranged
  A game at Rugby football.

In flaming jerseys starred and barred,
  They ranged themselves for action,
A team of charming Tory blue
  Opposed the Liberal faction.

Then to it tooth and nail they went
  Was never such a melly,
They beat each other black and blue
  Upon the sea-beach shelly.

The Frenchies gathered, wondering, round,
  Gesticulating, bustling,
And tried to learn from what arose
  The carnage and the tussling.

Meantime the players punched and pushed,
  Threw, butted, made the row too,
That only English football mad,
  (The Rugby game) know how to.

"And what is all the fight about?
  And what's that egg-like thick ball?"
"The English are enjoying, Sir,
  A quiet game at kickball."

And as he spoke a stretcher bore
  A player from the scrimmages,
And damaged worse were several more
  Than ancient Grecian images.

And when the gentle game was done
  The rival teams were plastered
With mud and slush from top to toe—
  The masters and the mastered.

And one had ricked his shoulder-blade,
  On head and limbs were patches
Where hair and skin had given way,
  And all had wounds and scratches.

"Such scenes," the Frenchy said (Away
  He turned), "should not be lawful,
If that is how the English play,
  Their fighting must be awful!"

WHAT DEATH SAID.

GRIM Death of yore a bright scythe bore
  Through hamlet, grove, and town,
And when he saw a likely stalk
  He promptly mowed it down.

The crops now drop themselves. No need
  Of scythe. He tried to sell
The thing, but failed, so broke it up
  And flung it down a well.

I met him once by Weston Brook,
  No wrap or paint disguised him,
Still, carrying neither scythe nor glass,
  I had not recognised him.

He stopped me, wished not to intrude;
  It took away my breath
When, button-holing me he said;
  "My card—my name is Death.

"In ancient days, if God's sweet air
  Through casement came or rafts
They welcomed in the atmosphere,
  But now you brand it 'draughts.'

"You now, I find, year in year out
  Inter yourselves in tombs
Some eight feet square, for hours and hours—
  I mean your stuffy rooms.

"Your doors, you sandbag, fasten baize
  Wherever there may be hole,
You paper every slit and crack,
  And plug the dangerous keyhole.

"And thus you live in atmosphere
  Oppressive, foul, and fetid,
Your faces lose the rosy tint
  Of health; and yet they're heated.

"I hate you doughy, milk faced things,
  And yet I love you, too,
For if you took the air, small work
  Were left for me to do.

"Which would be bad for my dear wife,
  My little Cains and Seths,
When Father Death is out of work,
  There's nought for little Deaths.

"You blanch and shrink if chance you see
    A coffin. Each one stives
In stuffy rooms, you really live
    In coffins all your lives.

"Go out and share God's blessed air,
    Or, if you can't, stay in,
But open throw the sash, and let
    It come to you. You sin

"By night and day. In summer gay,
    In winter bleak and bare,
Drink deep, and spare not—do not sip—
    The precious, sweet, fresh air,

"Don't scream at little puffs and draughts,
    Like school girl at a mouse,
And don't entomb your stuffy self
    Within your stuffy house!

"But I, what am I saying, Ah!
    I'm mad!"   He paused for breath.
"I've gone and let the secret out.
    Adieu. My name is Death."

4th October, 1896.

THE YEAR BEGINS WITH YELLOW.

THE year begins with yellow,
    There's the primrose in the frith,
The crowfoot and the daffodil,
    And the celandine by every rill—
    You know the swallow myth.

The year declines with yellow,
    You have seen the autumn trees,
The aspen clumps are as gold piled high,
    And the elm trees yellow the very sky,
    And shame the Hesperides.

HE PREFERRED THEM SEPARATELY

As in my den I sat, a friend
Amused herself by singing
And playing the piano. Then
The church bells started ringing.
Pianofortes are very well,
And so are bells ; but lately
I've got to think that I prefer
Their music separately.

As if the twain were not enough,
The baby started crying;
Two noises at a time may charm,
But three are rather trying.
I like a song, I like the bells,
I like the baby greatly,
(It's weak of me, I know), but I
Prefer them separately.

18th September, 1896.

I CAN WAIT

Or what Alexander Pope said at Twenty.

" *Well, for the future, I'll drown all high thoughts in the Lethe of
Cowslip Wine." Letter of* 1oth *May,* 1708.

HONOURS do not come to me,
Spiteful Fortune sneers, and lays
On another's head the bays :
Let her, none can strip the tree—
I can wait.

Riches do not come to me,
But I've fuel and a bed,
Pens, and a roof-tree over-head,
Health, and an acre or two may-be—
I can wait.

Fame I craved of all things here
Turns on me her back. Heigho !
I ? I turn my back also,
Scorn for scorn, and jeer for jeer !
I can wait.

MAKE UP YOUR MIND.

In doubt whene'er put up a prayer,
 Then strike, for you will find
That the greatest good is to do and dare—
 Make up your mind.

For men uncertain, wavering, weak,
 There is no spot on earth's round rind.
Decide : and Greek confronting Greek,—
 Make up your mind.

Rebuffs, what though like hail they whiz,
 Those pellets from a foe unkind,
He scarcely feels whose motto is—
 Make up your mind.

DUHESME AT PESCARA. *

An incident taken from the Memoirs of General Thiebault.

" And who commands the fortalice ? "—
 " The Marquis."—" Is he hale ?
How old ? "—" Say Seventy "—" Stout, robust ? "—
 " No, thin and very pale."—
" Much hair ? "—" Some little powdered curls.
 To Fashion, Sir, he truckles."—
" Wears boot and spur ? "— " Silk stockings, Sir,
 And shoes with monster buckles."—
" Advance, the place is mine, Ah, ah !
 Big buckles !" laughed our leader,
" Dame Fashion's slaves were never match
 For men who do not heed her."

20th October, 1896.

THE TREES ARE CHANGING COLOUR.

"The trees are changing colour,"
 He murmured slowly, sadly.
" You always would have summer then ? "—
 "Assuredly and gladly."

" Skies always blue, trees ever green,
 And sunshine every day !
The very thought's enough to blanch
 One's cheek, and strike dismay.

* The defender of Pescara was the Marquis of Pietramaggiore.

" I like your clear, cerulean sky,
    Your green umbrageous vista,
But give me, for a change, dark clouds,
    And branches bare and bistre ;
" The times and seasons as they pass
    Mild, torrid, balmy, freezing,
Give, Sir, to me variety—
    Perspiring, shivering, sneezing,
" Sun, snow, and rain, and north-east wind—
    Eat always, sir, of one tree ?
Why, were our climate changed for you
    I'd leave the wretched country."

29th September, 1896.

EARLY MORNING.

Written at the Ferry near the Waterworks, Bedford.

SWEET breezes the orchard trees blew on,
Her fillet and wimple she drew on,
    Roved early and basked in the sunshine of morn,
Her breakfast ripe fruit with the dew on.

Oh, give me the morning for musing,
The fresh, early dawn is my choosing,
    When grass, bird, and insect are o'er again born.
Why will you such pleasures be losing !

The catkins depend from the willows,
Renounce, drowsy maidens, your pillows,
    The east is all jacinth, and crimson, and fawn,
And the forest tops wanton like billows.

Hark, hark, to the chains of the ferry,
They blend with the antiphon merry
    Of finches who flit, with chirrup and twit,
Round wheatear, and blossom, and berry.

Approaches a weather-worn drover,
His bootlaces soaked by the clover,
    He handles the chain ; comes the music again
As he leisurely pulls himself over.

The stream with the laughing sun brightens,
The age-doddered willow-tree whitens,
   The scene is more fair than Berenice's hair,[1]
Or a Venus attended by Tritons.

So soft are the zephers and balmy.
The poets, a petulant army,
   Praise highly the day when old Saturn held sway ;
To doubt if that era were palmy

Were heresy grossly pernicious ;
But join me some morning delicious
   And we'll enter again a Saturnian reign
More suave than Parnassus could wish us.

THE TYRANNY OF PRINT.

Written on reading, in a lecture by Mr. W. R. Hughes, that Herbert Spencer, when a boy " actually declined to accept statements, although they appeared in printed books."

OF Jinn[2] and anthropophagi[3]
   The world has still no stint,
But what can wield the evil eye
   Or eat men up like Print ?

We read some man's opinion
   Embalmed in white and black
And we are that man's minion,
   His dinner, or his hack.

Shall any merely mortal
   To us be " Great Apollo " ?
Shall we through every portal
   His curlëd finger follow ?

" Good gracious, no ! " says Spencer
   " No matter who he be,
Wit, prophet, poet, censor,
   His gospel were to me

No more than wind and bladder,
   Were nought persuasive in't,"
(" Oh wiser man and sadder.")
   "Although it stood in print."

1 Berenice's. Four syllables, accent on second.
2 Evil spirits.
3 Cannibals,

THE QUARREL FOR MOTHER.

Related by Samuel Ploughman, youngest son of Mr. Jonathan Ploughman, farmer.

WHEN father died—or I should have said,
When the doctor gave him up for dead—
My father's sons, there were four with me,
As fine young men as you e'er did see,
Though I say it myself—broad chest, strong limb—
My father was tall, but we all topped him,
My father's sons, John, James, and Joe,
And Sam, that's me, in the room below,
Were sitting, so gloomy and silent, all four,
When Mary, the servant, threw open the door.
The hem of her apron was fast to her eye,
At first she could nothing but stutter and cry;
And then, with the tear drops her good face upon,
She told us, all sobbing, that father was gone.

We thought of dear father, devoted and kind,
And then of poor mother left helpless behind;
Our hearts were all aching—and deep in my breast
Rose a thought, and the same filled the hearts of the rest.
At first in our sorrow, there followed a dead,
Deep silence.   Then John broke the silence, and said—
"Though grieved my dear brothers, though grieved to the core,
Yet now seems the time to decide—I am sure
You know what I mean.   'Twould be fair as can be
For me to have mother.   I hope you'll agree,
For, being the eldest, I have the first claim;
If you were the eldest, why, you'd say the same."

"Hold, hold!" blurted James; "it must not be so,
For mother will need to be strengthened you know,
And, seeing my home's in a town by the sea,
'Twould be better by far to give mother to me."

"Very good, brother James, then we'll let her go down,
And stay for a month, or two months, in your town;
Will you promise," said John, "on your honour," said he,
As soon as she's well to return her to me?"

But James shook his head, and full firmly said, "Nay,"
For he wanted her all to himself.   Lack-a-day!

I tremble to think how the quarrel had closed,
When suddenly Joe, that's the next, interposed.
" My brothers," said he, "Nay, don't scowl or look glum,
Annoyed and impatient, till now I've been dumb,
But all of you, yes every one, must admit
That nothing more sensible could be, more fit,
Than mother—how all of us love her!—to which
Of her sons should she go, but the one that is rich!
I cast no reflections " (he'd manners, had Joe),
" But I, as the twain of you very well know,
Have money, and acres, and houses; I'm loath
To say it, but well I could buy up you both.
So make no more quibble or pother," said he,
" But quietly hand over mother to me."

But scarce had he finished, my rich brother Joe,
When, my heart all a bursting to hear him talk so,
I cried : "Though your meaning is good, just a word,
For I, though the youngest, yet I must be heard.
'Tis true I'm the youngest—the babe if you choose—
Though I stand six feet one and a half in my shoes."
(I blubbered, and looked mighty foolish I know),
" But *I* want her too ; give her *me*."   "Nay," said Joe,
Nor would he give way, and James he was mad
At being so thwarted, and John was as bad,
And crosser, yes crosser, if crosser could be,
Than Joe was, or James was, or Sam was—that's me.

And no one need wonder to find us so sore,
For a mother like ours was ne'er heard of before,
Not peevish, or selfish, and not hard to please,
Not cross, discontented, or fond of her ease,
But gentle, hard working, kind, thoughtful, and good,
Who each of us just like a book, understood.
Who did, who did everything mothers should do,
The like I ne'er heard of, no never, did you ?
Well, John, he looked black, and James heaved a sigh,
And Joe he looked daggers at John, so did I,
And John he looked daggers at Joe and at me,
And I was as unked as unked could be :
When lo ! the door opened, the girl must be mad !
For there we saw Mary not weeping or sad,
But her face beaming joy—not a tear to be seen.
We stared, what on earth could the change in her mean !

"Thank God! oh, thank God"—it was all she could say,
At first—then succeeded " Oh, happy the day !
My master, your father, yet lives, joy to tell,
And more, says the doctor, he'll some day be well!"

'Twas true, down and down, till they thought he was dead
Poor father had sunk ; but when life was nigh fled
He suddenly rallied, the crisis, the pain
Were gone ; and God gave us our father again.
The thanks and rejoicings 'twould tire you to tell,
Suffice it to say that dear father got well.
And thus the great quarrel among us begun
Was ended. None ended so happily. None
Could now feel offended. Offended? Oh, no.
We wept for delight, but 'twould not have been so
Had father not rallied—for how heal the sore
Since mother could not be divided in four?
And what other way a solution to find
I know not, for none ever entered my mind.

But now, all as happy as mortals below
Can possibly be, every day to and fro
Passed presents and compliments. John, it was he
Made a start, bought a heavy gold watch chain for me,
And I, before putting the said watch chain on,
Went and purchased a new silk umbrella for John.
And Joe unto James gave a hat, be it said,
A hat, by the way, far too large for his head ;
And James, not his brother to pain, I suppose,
Though the brim of it pressed on the ridge of his nose,
Assured the kind donor it suited him so
That whene'er it was worn 'twould remind him of Joe.
And James in return gave—but there, I am sure
You'd only be bored—we were happy all four.

And so that our friendliness ne'er might be rent,
Dear father one evening the whole of it spent,
And a day or two after, in making his will.
And these were the words, I remember them still,
I, Jonathan Ploughman, in sound state of mind
(For which God be praised), I am leaving behind
A wife I love dearly—my sons four they be,
But the one she's to live with is—well, let me see.
With John? But the rest would object. Well, with Joe?
I could'nt give pain to his brothers, oh, no!

With Sam ?   What would John say ?   With James—worser
   still—
It's plaguey hard business this making a will."
He mused for a moment, he thought the thing o'er,
He gazed on the ceiling, he gazed on the floor,
"There's one way, and only one way, I can find,
To settle the matter at all to their mind
(As the ink and the paper he placed on the shelf)
" I must live and take care of their mother myself."
He said it, 'tis easy to say it, you'll say,
But he stuck to his text, and he's living to-day.

THE FRIAR AND THE SHOES.

John the Friar, as his order bade,
Gear for foot had never had ;
But, walking out, on the dusty ground
A very good pair of shoes he found,
And thinking it pity to leave them, John
Picked up the shoes and put them on,
Turned in home, his prayers he said in them,
Ate his crust, and went to bed in them.
But never had man such an awful night,
Thieves leaped in with daggers bright,
" Kill, kill, kill !"—" A Friar am I !"—
" Nay, for you're shod.   Base man, you lie !"—
" Look at my foot," and he raised it, " do !"
   Then he awoke—and the shoes were there,
Each plump foot had its neat, sleek shoe.
   Stung with remorse, he seized the pair
And both away in the midnight threw.
Bare now his feet as his tonsured crown,
But his heart is light as thistle-down,
And, since, he has seen no spectral sight,
And never been plagued with one bad night ;
But it does not follow that if *you* lose
Your sleep you'd better destroy *your* shoes,
Or that if you do, when your shoes are gone
You'll sleep like a top, or like Friar John.

MATRIMONY.

I ONCE dictated to my boys
  A page that none had seen,
But whether from delightful Froude,
  I cannot say, or Green.

King Henry, having much admired
  Sweet Katharine's visage sunny,
Her sunnier dowry entered on,
  And into matrimony.

Then, going round, I raised a slate
  To see the writing better,
"A capital?" I asked, "Why spell
  The word with that sized letter?"—

"As into matrimony, Sir,
  They entered," (looking down)
"I put a capital because
  I thought it was a town."—

"And very true, a large one too,
  And that there's no denying
Though some (We cannot blink the fact)
  Have found its climate trying,

"But some declare they like its air;
  That it agrees with them,
But either way they have to stay—
  We use a little 'm.'"

                    6th October, 1896.

NEVER BE SATISFIED WITH ANYTHING AT ALL.

A LETTER once keen Franklin wrote—
  "Try, try," observed the writer,
"My lad, you are on orders bent
  So level at a mitre."

But why a limit? My advice
  Were sounder: "Chappie small,
Try, try; but ne'er be satisfied
  With anything at all."

BREAKING UP SONG.

Tune : " Come, let us raise a merry song."

Now's the time for laugh and song,
No-one's face to-day is long,
None to-day will moan or sigh,
Hang the head or pipe the eye.
   Ha, Ha, Ha, etc. (*Clap hands*).

What a jolly time's in store :
Crackers, forfeits, nuts galore,
Story books with tales that please,
Mistletoe and Christmas trees.

We shall slide, and we shall race,
Until each vermilion face
Flames enough—did one but try—
To ignite a candle by.

Good bye copy-books and slates,
Now for jolly walks and skates,
Brims with joyfulness our cup,
Hip, hurrah ! we're breaking up.

Good bye teachers, lessons, too,
Malice none we bear to you,
But a change is good for each—
Those who learn and those who teach.

Fathers, mothers, sisters small,
Merry Christmas to you all !
Happy days and rattling fun,
Hip, hurrah ! for every one.

PLUNGE IN THE DARK.

How strange, how various are the moods that can
Assert themselves, and be displayed in man !
To-day, with heated brow, and flashing eyes,
His soul all fire, he presses to the prize.
The goal he sees, and nought obstructs his pride
But what, impetuous, he whirls aside ;
To-morrow, beaten, broken, bowed, depressed,
He sees no way, no path, no course ; the rest

Of this life's journeyings can only be
One line of failure and of misery—
And all because some trifle unforeseen
Doth for the moment interpose between
His mark and him.   Disprove it if you can,
Both strange and various are the moods of man.

To-day, industrious, he plods and gains—
Some inches, still they're inches, for his pains,
But more than this, at night he sinks to rest
Conscious at least of having tried his best,
Of having done, delightful words and true,
As much as holiest seraphim can do.
Happy, serene—with tired brain and limb,
If aught I covet 'tis the sleep of him.

To-morrow, dallying with that or this
The hours have vanished ere their owner is
Aware, and when at last aware, he takes
The pen, with thoughts unconcentrate, he makes
But feeble effort.   "What is this I do?"
He asks, " And what about the end in view!
What chance is there, what hope presents, that it
Can be attained?"   Why none if thus you sit.
Work on; the men who hum and hesitate
Until the path is clear will always wait.

What work, achievement, anything by man
Accomplished, was what when that work began
Its author yearned for, or at last was done
Conformably to primal planning?—None.
Wish nothing definite, but ceaseless try
With ardour burning, aspirations high,
Plunge in the dark as if it were the sun,
'Tis thus, exactly, every man has done.
Of your own future be assured of this
You know as much as any man of his,
As much as any man (why then forlorn!)
Ere knew of his, that ever yet was born.[1]

---

[1] It is certainly startling to be reminded that there were times when Shakspere, Napoleon, Robert Stephenson, and all other eminent men, did not know that they would be able to accomplish anything in particular.

TWO HEROES.

Julius Cæsar and St. Francis.

1.—*Cæsar.*

THE name of Cæsar hangs upon our lips,
Ashore he leads us, and with him in ships
We cross the main.   His frequent wars recur,
His high ambition.   Mid the angry stir
Of those hot ferments of distracted Rome
He moves resourceful.   See him far from home
In Gaul, in Swabia, on the sands of Kent,
Wherever foe or cruel faction spent
Its hopeless fury.   Neither doubted he,
Whate'er the peril, his high destiny.
Distrustful never of himself he spent,
No foolish hours in anxious discontent :
Where'er we view him, in whatever state,
His aim was single, and his purpose great !
The goal is gained !   What though so short his day !
And Casca's dagger found so soon its prey !
His aim was empire.   Rome had many a son
But such ambition fevered only one ;
One only dared to nurture in his breast
Such aspirations.   They are always blest—
The brave and bold !   And fortune favours still
The pertinacious.   Cæsar had his will.

2.—*St. Francis.*

WHAT sight is this ! a youth of noble mien
In rags unsightly by the rabble seen,
Pelted, and jeered at, sought by shameful cries—
A strange fire burning in his ardent eyes.
O pure St. Francis, as we read we seem
Ourselves to catch a few small rays, a gleam
Of that strange fire, and we too something feel
Of thy unwearied, thy resistless zeal,
Thy deafness to the world's poor, paltry cry,
The ardour keen, the aspirations high ;
Something of thy enthusiastic fires
Kindles in us, we too have fierce desires,
And we would conquer.   Ever saintly man,
Thy shade replies, " Who wills to conquer can."

The scene at Rome.   Seraphic Francis went
For papal benediction and consent
That, though the humblest of the humble, he
Might form and fire a great fraternity
Of starveling workers like himself, all bent
On saving souls.   At first astonishment
Transfixed the pope, arrayed in scarlet dress,
And gems and gold.   Before this gorgeousness
In rags he stood, but nothing thought of this
So full was he of his high purposes.

'Twas not all haughtiness, and pomp, and pride,
That swayed the pope, his sympathies were wide,
And in the peasant's earnest way and word
Something that differed from the common herd
He saw, and seeing it, the boon conferred.
'Twas thus in distant, mediaeval days
St. Francis work began.   A halo plays
About his life and teaching.   Mid the night
Of force and violence, he gleams a bright—
A single meteor.   'Tis a wondrous tale,
The story of his work, and words would fail
To tell his labours, of the good that came,
And the great order that assumed his name.

SAINT DEFOE.

'TIS understood that some prefer
    A tranquil life and quiet,
But others revel, like Defoe,
    In racket, stir, and riot.
Like wanton boy, the hornets' nests
    He tickled with his bludgeon,
He gave the grave dissenters pokes,
    He raised the High Church dudgeon.
He shrieked, lampooned, he bit the thumb,
    And corrugated brow,
To-day he cuffs Sacheverell,
    To-morrow pummels Howe.
He jibed at Swift, he libelled Pope,
    At Dryden had his fling,
And into solemn Addison
    Injected deep his sting ;

And when in agony they writhed
And turned upon the Tartar,
He nimbly popped his nimbus on
And posed The Blessed Martyr.

17th October, 1896.

POEMS FROM MY NOVELS.

"THE WELLS"
Or Tunbridge Wells in the days of Queen Anne.

From " The Knight o' the Post."

OH do you know the Wells, good Sir,
  Do you affect thę Wells?
And do you dote on furbelows,
  On hoops and red heeled belles?
And is it your delight to stroll
  With sword-knot[1] to your knees
If wet below the portico,
  If fine beneath the trees?

I met her near the Assembly Room
  All blooming, bright, cerise,
" What you!" said I. " Oh ay," said she.
  We walked beneath the trees.
" My health," said she—" but then, you know,
  That nothing can repair
A shattered constitution like
  The Tunbridge wells and air.

" And Tunbridge is a pleasant place
    As far as medicine goes
And excellent the recipe
    Of darling Dr. Rose[2]
'Tis true I do not follow it—
    The twenty pints a day—
With me a sip is quite enough
    To drive all ills away.

"The waters drunk, 'tis angling time
    For charming girls, well dressed ;
And bachelors (with pockets)
    Are always in request ;
There's courting and flirtation,
    And each a dancing goes,
And basset for proprietors
    Of old and tender toes.

1 Sword knots of gay colour, worn very long, were fashionable.
2 A Tunbridge celebrity who prescribed twenty pints of the waters daily.

" But I'm sure you know the Wells, good Sir,
    Of course you know the Wells,
You could not, no one can resist,
    Its hooped and red heeled belles ;
And passing pleasant 'tis to stroll
    With sword-knot to your knees,
If wet below the portico,
    If fine beneath the trees."

AT LINTOT'S ON THE ICE.*

From " The Knight o' the Post."

* In the time of Queen Anne the Thames was frozen over, and many tradesmen
including the great booksellers, had stalls on the ice.

LET others waste the precious hours
    That make up human life
In hockey, skating, quoits or mall—
    Your dolts are always rife,
Alack !—Such sports are not for me,
    They please me not at all,
But oh, the joy of brooding o'er
    The books on Lintot's stall !

How could I waste my precious hours,
    That swift as arrows go,
In hurling like a very boy
    A ball of frozen snow."—
" This Hobbes marked fourpence."—" Eh ? an eight !
    My eyes are weak, I know't.
We'll split the difference ?   Won't you ?   Ah !
    Well there's the other groat.
" And this is ? "—" Fippence."—" Thank you.   That."
    " A shilling."—" Yon in blue ? "
"A tester."—" If you'll throw it in
    I'll take the other two."
" I can't afford it."—" Can't you."—" I've
    A wife and children three—
            (*Aside.*)
(And eighty thousand all put out
    On good security.")

'Twas thus we haggled on the ice
  The spluttering put[1] and I,
But luck'ly for my purse that day
  I did not care to buy.
I said, " Adieu," and turned to go.
  " Stop, stop ! I'll take your price,"
And so we came to terms, you see
  At Lintot's on the ice.

MY LOVE A BOOK.

From "The Knight o' the Post."

To what shall I liken my darling's face—
  To a priceless book ? Beloved let
Thy cheeks be the soft morocco case,
  Thine eyes the gems in the binding set,

Thine ears the delicate ivory plaques,
  And thy brow the ivory, too, like snow ;
Thy hair is the marker ravelled out,
  Of softest silk, and gold also.

Thy lips are the soft, raised ruby rests
  With the title on so fairly writ,
Thy mind is the beautiful text within,
  And the Master above hath printed it.

ST. DUNSTAN.

The Blacksmith's song in "The Mystery of St. Dunstan's."

St. Dunstan of old had a brawny arm,
He could sing with the best his godly psalm,
And his tuneful hammer fell and rose
And the anvil answered his measured blows :
There's nothing, you'll find, on land or sea
Like muscle allied with piety.

To his sweet-toned harp St. Dunstan sang,
And the notes in the high-roofed chancel rang,
They rippled, and quivered, and floated on,
And angels carolled the antiphon ;
Oh, nothing you'll find on land or sea,
Like muscle, and music, and piety.

[1] Dr. Young called Lintot " a great spluttering fellow." " Put," eighteenth century, for a clumsy looking fellow.

'Tis told in the field, 'tis told in the town,
How he drew the designs for my lady's gown,
How he loved, how he painted, and carved, and prayed,
And ghost after ghost securely laid:
There's nothing like love on land or sea,
And muscle, and music, and piety.

St. Dunstan's name to his church shall cling,
St Dunstan's fame shall the choirmen sing,
His windows and bells—may their glories last!
The sweet-toned bells that St. Dunstan cast:
There's nothing like art on land or sea,
Love, music, and muscle and piety.

It was Dunstan's method of doing things,
He struck off crowns, and he set up kings;
But only kings who could understand,
That the actual man who ruled the land,
Loved music and art.   Fair things they be:
Love, energy, muscle, and piety.

" He tinkered the laws, he righted wrongs,
And someone has cause to remember his tongs,
'Tis a ticklish task to take kings by the heel,
But who but a Dunstan had tackled the deil!
Art, music, and will, fair things they be,
Love, energy, muscle, and piety."

AT " THE FOLLY " ON THE THAMES.

From " The Mystery of St. Dunstan's."

" The Folly " was an immense Pleasure Boat moored in the middle of the Thames
—time of Queen Anne.

OH come unto the *Folly*,
    Ye beaux and ladies gay,
In silks and satins whiling
    The soft, warm hours away;
Delicious breezes fan you,
    And strains seductive float
In shallop come, or wherry
    Or fairy-fashioned boat.

"The streamers on the *Folly*
    Unfold them to the breeze,
And the rippling waters ravish
    Like singing birds in trees;
Oh, love delights in beauty,
    In 'witching scene and sound,
In the blue, bright sky arched over,
    The blue, bright waters round.

"Oh, pleasant is the *Folly*,
    Lament, sweet sirs, no more,
The commonplace existence,
    Ye lead on either shore ;
Here, lapped in sweetest music,
    Delightsome scenes ye view,
Ye dream yourselves in Eden
    And wake to find it true.

"Then come unto the *Folly*,
    Ye beaux and ladies gay,
In silks and satins whiling
    The soft, warm hours away ;
Delicious breezes fan you,
    And strains seductive float,
In shallop come, or wherry,
    Of fairy-fashioned boat."

THE CORNCRAKE.

The song of Doll Rainbow.

In " The Mystery of St. Dunstan's."

WHEN a simple child in my snowy bed,
    It was sometimes a trouble to me,
That when I would sleep I could not sleep
    For the corncrake in the lea.*
For the crake, crake, crake, crake
    Of the corncrake in the lea.

* The corncrake is heard all the summer long, in the meadows near Olney.

But many a night since then has flown,
    Of wickedness, sorrow, and dread,
And oft, full oft, I have lain awake,
But not through the cry of the grey corncrake
    As of old in my snowy bed,
The crake, crake, crake, crake,
    As of old in my snowy bed.

And oft, when tossing on my couch,
    And sleep would not come to me
I have wished it was only the grey corncrake,
    The corncrake in the lea,
The crake, crake, crake, crake
    Of the corncrake in the lea.

APPLE-TIME.

From "The Knight o' the Post."

THE world may wag, the world may mag,
    The river may sink to the sea,
The carter's wain may crawl to the town,
    Or anywhere else for me ;
For it's apple time, and the apples are red,
    And ripe on every tree.

In Crawley mead were twenty cows,
    I asked not what might ail
My Stella when her beauteous cheek
    So suddenly grew pale,
For every cow among them whisked
    Her formidable tail.

It wandered—my protecting arm—
    Around—I bade her mark
That near to me she was quite as safe
    As Noah in the ark,
"Then let them whisk their tails," I cried,
    " In orchard, mead, or park."

We sat beneath a hornbeam hedge,
    The sky above was blue,
A beetle came with feelers black
    And wings of golden hue,
And straight towards my darling's foot
    The dangerous creature flew.

My hand was down, it took its flight
 Among the apple trees,
The sunflowers shone, the marigolds blazed,
 And drowsily hummed the bees,
And me-thought it was the garden
 Of the famed Hesperides.

Her breath was sweet as straw of wheat,
 Her mouth was sweet likewise,
And now and then I pressed her lips,
 To keep away the flies,
For in apple-time they settle so
 On mouth, and nose, and eyes.

What more? A question, and a "yes,"
 Her eyes she dared not raise,
How swiftly apple-time used to go,
 But now for 'hours' read 'days,'
And months, and years, for two are one,
 And its apple-time now always!

POEMS ADDRESSED TO FRIENDS.

A WELCOME TO CANON BENHAM.

15th May, 1893.

FROM London's heat we welcome you
    To Olney's cooler air,
Our limpid streams and shady trees
    With you 'twere sweet to share,
But if it does not matter, pray,
    Good Canon, pick a Saturday.

From Monday's dawn to Friday's dusk
    To us pertain the joys,
Of filling up the sieve-like heads
    Of frisky girls and boys,
Who (Well their mothers know it) stay
    At home the whole of Saturday.

And you and I (delightful thought),
    Will saunter down and up
The fields by him of Olney sung,
    And to the dregs our cup,
Delirious we will drink, and say :
    " When was there such a Saturday !"

And I will show my dove-house quaint,
    And thatched, and round, and old,
And we will talk (how we will talk !),
    But if I'm not too bold,
And if it does not matter, pray,
    Good Canon, choose a Saturday.

TO MY FRIEND MR. W. R. HUGHES.
Treasurer of the City of Birmingham.

January, 1895.

Written after a visit to him at Handsworth. With recollections of his family,
his books, his horse and his dog.

DEAR host, and ever valued friend,
Our union death alone shall rend.
At first when I your treasures saw
I wished that I were you.   Before

The word escaped it dawned on me
That, metamorphosed, I should be
Not I, but you, and thus should lose
A right warm-hearted friend named Hughes.
And if he's mine each sumptuous prize
He, owns, of course, is mine likewise.
Heaven grant keen joy, and length of life
To you, your sons, and genial wife,
And daughters. Ah, your books ! Without them
You could not live ; I dream about them.
In short, I'd have you understand
We love you all, and grasp each hand,
And, none to slight beneath your roof,
We grasp likewise each paw and hoof.

TO MR. W. R. HUGHES.

On the occasion of the Marriage of his daughter Emily.

DEAR Dickens-lover, Spencer's friend,
The paragraph from end to end
We read.   We opened wide your door
And in imagination saw
 The guests, the gifts, and all beside.
 I would congratulate the bride,
   But I
   Am shy.

I've daughters of my own, and so
What daughters are precisely know ;
They're apt, affectionate, and sweet,
And fragranter than straw of wheat—
 A statement no one would deride.
 I would congratulate the bride,
   But I
   Am shy.

The wife she'll make ?   As if one could
Be aught but sensible and good
From home like yours ; attached to Naden,
Dickens and Spencer (thoughtful maiden)
 With sympathies so deep and wide.
 I would congratulate the bride,
   But I
   Am shy.

To lose a daughter, let me own,
Is like to losing limb or bone.
But if by happy wedlock's tether
The case is different altogether,
 One's tears may then be brushed aside.
I would congratulate the bride,
        But I
        Am shy.

Congratulations! God above
Knows how we honour you and love,
And for your sake, if for no other,
Including (That's of course), her mother,
 May joy the wedded pair betide.
I would congratulate the bride,
        But I
        Am shy.

18th September, 1896.

TO PHILIP, WITH A NEW PEN.

(The world is my oyster.—Falstaff.)

PHILIP, this oyster world is closed,
 But to you I commit,
This pen, and with its steely point
 I bid you open it.
But should the weapon not suffice,
 Take axe, or saw, or plough;
So only you the valves displace
 It matters little how.

29th March 1896.

TO CHRISTABEL.

FOUR at Christmas, rather fair,
 Let me bend and twine,
Learn of me, for whatsoe'er
 I possess is thine.

O thou loved Intelligence,
 Eyes so bright and blue,
Be to me " Great Babylon,"*
 I'll be king to you.

October, 1896.

* " Is not this great Babylon that I have built ? "   Daniel IV., 30.

POEMS WRITTEN FOR MY SCHOLARS.

BUNYAN'S CHRISTMAS.

Tune : Good King Wencelas.

THICKLY fell the Christmas snow,
　　Drifting into hollows,
Merry skaters down below
　　Skimmed the ice like swallows ;
Rose the prisoner from his book,
　　Peeped without his grating,
For it almost warmed to look
　　Down upon the skating.*

" Would," said he, " this stiffened limb
　　I could chafe out yonder."
Cried the jailer, kind but grim,
　　" Well you do to ponder,
Think it out—the word to me
　　Give—by next assizes
We could part, and you be free
　　Like yon snipe that rises."

" Nay, if I may not proclaim
　　Christ the slain and risen—
Better shackles far than shame—
　　Freedom would be prison.
Still my thoughts can roan." He turned
　　Unto pen and paper,
And into the starred night burned
　　Long his humble taper.

Burdened Christian mends his ways,
　　Leaves his squalid alley,
Tumbles in the Slough, displays
　　Valour in the Valley ;

---

* Skates had at this time only recently been introduced from Holland.

F

Fierce Apollyon, net and noose,
    Giant, cheat and lion
Frustrates ; fords the final Ouse,
    Enters dazzling Zion.

When at last the work is done,
    Stands the saint elated,
Still aglow the sliders run,
    Still the skaters skated ;
Futile 'gainst the mind is force,
    None can bind or link her,
Witness all, the Pilgrim's course
    Pictured by the Tinker.

                        9th Nov. 1896.

I WON'T BE A DUNCE.

Tune : I won't be a nun.

Now is it not a pity such an active girl as I
Should so much time have wasted ? But now I mean to try ;
    For I won't be a dunce, No, I won't be a dunce,
    I'll never more be idle, for I won't be a dunce.

I cannot bear that others should get in front of me,
It makes me Turkey-red with shame, and green with jealous y
    So I, &c.

Besides when you grow older,—it is the whole world's way—
The dunces do the drudgery, the skilled ones take the pay ;
    So I, &c.

I've quite a thousand chances more than girls that I could name,
And if I don't advantage take, there'll be but one to blame ;
    So I, &c.

Besides how very sweet is play when you have worked with will,
I'm gaining, but I mean to get a good deal higher still ;
    So I, &c.

And happier then my mother and teachers will be far
Than bull-finches and sparrows in gooseberry bushes are ;
    So I, &c.

And folks will say, " Is this the girl that never used to strive,
And always was so ignorant ? Why bless my heart alive !"
    So I, &c.

OUR SCHOOL.

Tune : John Peel.

Do you know our school, with its desks and maps,
And the books that crowd all the shelves and gaps ?
Have you seen our bags with neat spruce straps,
     And the slates that we fill in the morning ?
For we're very, very busy all the day inside,
And to keep clean books is our aim and pride,
But we shout Hurrah! when we get outside
     And lessons are done for the morning.

Yes, I know your school and your teacher too,
For she once drilled me as she now drills you,
And if what she says is precisely true
     You've worked very well all the morning.
Dear me, your cheeks are like logs at Yule,
Your bright eyes gleam like a sunlit pool,
So here's Hurrah for yourselves and the school,
     And the lessons you learn in the morning.

We like our French with its Parlez vous,
We like our Latin with its Hic, Hac, too,
And perhaps you would glance at the maps that we drew,
     And the sums that we worked in the morning.
We like to drill and we like to sew,
And when visitors come we stand in row
And figures and cards and copybooks show,
     And the maps that we do in the morning.

My friends, I hear that you love your books,
And never say can't or show glum looks,
Or spurtle with ink-drops black as rooks
     Your pinafores clean in the morning,
So I've asked if for once you may have more play,
And a half day off this very fine day,
So now Hurrah ! for I'm sure that you'll say
     "We'll work all the more every morning."

SAVED FROM A BULL.

A True Story.

THAT great jail wall at Bedford—
  Could blanker, gloomier be !—
E'en now whene'er I pass it
  My legs sink under me.

My boy was home returning,
  Lest older lads should greet him
And tease, as was their custom,
  I went that day to meet him.

Well, just as he had reached the jail
  He spied me, called out "Mother";
I see him now that side the road,
  For I was on the other.

He ran to meet me. All at once
  There rose a hue and cry,
And then a fierce, enormous bull
  Dashed foaming, bellowing by.

My child flew back. Against the wall
  He stood—no nook to screen us.
I tried to reach my boy, the beast
  Dashed back again between us,

Its awful horns towards the ground.
  All round the folk came flocking,
It charged my poor defenceless child,
  The great horns pinned him. Shocking !

They tell me like a stone I dropped,
  Loud voices seemed to call me,
Pray God experience such as that
  May ne'er again befall me !

They say that when my sense returned
  I shrieked—they soothed in vain—
And called on God to save my boy,
  And swooned and swooned again.

Then on my lips and cheeks there fell,
  The warmth of loving kisses,
" Sweet mother, mother, I am safe,
  Your own dear chappie this is."

'Twas true, the horns had struck the wall
My boy was pinned,—a horn each side him—
Then down he slid; the bull was fixed
And soon the folk securely tied him.

Without a scratch! True tale, and thus
Did God my boy deliver,
E'en now I never pass that wall
Without a painful shiver.

28th Sept. 1896.

MAGIC-LANTERN LAND.

Written after giving a Lantern Entertainment, with the help of Mr. E. Sowman,
to my School Children, 20th Oct. 1896.

I KNOW a charming country
More fair than France or Spain,
And though I've often seen it
I'd like to go again;
But Cissy says she'd like to stay,
And never, never come away.

And in this charming country
Are views of Greece and Rome,
The grand St. Mark's of Venice,
And Omar's mosque and dome;
But Cissy likes the Moslem more
Who rolls his eyes and lifts his jaw.

And there's the spot in Bethlehem
Where Jesus Christ was born,
The Sultan's house (too good for him
I'm sure), at Golden Horn;
But Cissy wonders how they make
The steamers puff across the lake.

We saw the thieves attack the man
And leave him like to die,
The Levite and the heartless priest
Who passed the sufferer by;
And Cissy whispered in my ear
" I hope it's not the last or near."

We saw the man with mutton pies
　　Composed of pussy cats,
And, dear me! how we shrieked to see
　　The glutton swallow rats;
But Cissy twigged the whole concern,
She says she saw the handle turn.

You should have heard us clap our hands
　　To see poor Snoozer try
To catch—poor inoffensive man—
　　The aggravating fly;
Said Cissy " How his bald head rises!
The fly's too large by several sizes."

But oh, those donkeys at the stile!
　　That board with writing plain
Turned so that we could read it, " When
　　Shall we three meet again?"
And Cissy, turning to her mother,
Said " Two, I see, but where's the other?"

But when there came a shabby man
　　With coat and waistcoat white,
And long-haired brush, on arm a can,
　　And poster with "Good Night,"
From Cissy such a long long " Oh-h-h-h"
Escaped, and then we rose to go.

And Cissy wonders if the man
　　Who showed the pictures gay
Gives entertainments to himself
　　And children every day;
And if the people great and small
There ever go to bed at all.

But when they've done begin again
　　Like toper with his cup,
But said it very drowsily,
　　And propped her eyelids up;
But the miller scattered his dusty heap
And mother picked her up asleep.

NAPOLEON AND THE RABBITS.

Suggested by an incident recorded in the Memoirs of General Thiebault.

A DUKE, the great Napoleon,
  Addressed, one morning fine,
And said "Come, shoot my rabbits,
  And taste my crusted wine,
And, possibly, you'd honour me
  In my poor house to dine."

Then to his man (aside) " I want
  A thousand rabbits, get them,
My neighbours, if you tell my need,
  I'm sure will kindly net them.
And on that morning, in my woods,
  All loose of course you'll let them."

'Twas done. Towards the woods they strode.
  The walk and sunshine heat them,
No need to search for rabbits,
  The rabbits ran to meet them.
Napoleon stood amazed, the duke
  Used whip, and lashed and beat them.

But still they would not run away—
  At least not one in ten go—
They leaped between Napoleon's legs,
  Would not towards the glen go,
Not worse the general was bested
  By Melas at Marengo.

On hind legs now they pawed him.   Sure
  Was never such a pother,
They rummaged all his pockets, stood
  On top of one another,
And seemed to recognise in him
  A bosom friend and brother.

Napoleon now against a tree
  Stood gallantly at bay,
But still the rabbits threw themselves
  Like Austrians on their prey;
At last unto his heels he took
  And fairly ran away.

The rabbits followed. Then, by chance,
  A truck of cabbage passed.
The rabbits, letting go their prey,
  As sailors would a mast,
Swarmed up the truck. The secret,
  It seems, leaked out at last.

Imagining in rabbits
  The difference not much is,
The man, not from the warren got
  The beasts, but from the hutches.
(He took good care to keep that day
  Out of his master's clutches).

Thus tame ones had been brought. They all
  Mistook (Poor beasts deluded),
Napoleon for the cabbage man,—
  Or all except a few did.
Mistakes! We all have made mistakes,
  Dear reader, you included.

3rd Oct. 1896.

THE BOY WHO RAN AWAY TO SEA.

PLEASE tell me a tale.
  I'll tell you a tale,
And a strange one it shall be :
  There was once a boy named Bates,
  Who hated books and slates,
And one fine day he ran away to sea.

Said he " Good bye to sums,
  Good bye to inky thumbs,
And fingers, and to drawing stupid maps ;
  I'll sail to far Japan,
  And get to be a man,
And p'raps I'll be Mikado of the Japs."

But scarcely had he got
  A furlong from his cot
When lo ! a cow and calf approached to bar
  His way. Now it appears
  That cows are very fierce,—
But mothers plagued with babies mostly are.

Then said this urchin small
" I'll go back after all,
It seems that there are dangers in the way,
And I don't exactly see
How my mother without me
Could get along for even half a day.

"And sums are ne'er so long,
Or yet so very wrong
But you can do them if you try your best,
And do them one would rather
Than go some inches farther
And get a crooked cow-horn in your chest."

So back again he turned,
And home, again, he learned
That he had been away—this truant lad—
According to the tower
Great clock, just half an hour
And yet adventures perilous had had.

And so this little man
Has never reached Japan—
The land beyond the empire of the Czars—
But he's great at Long Division,
And speaks with much derision,
Of boys who cannot paraphrase or parse.

And more, his doting mother
Makes such a desperate pother
About his wondrous progress, so perhaps
She couldn't be much prouder,
Or boast about it louder,
If he'd got to be Mikado of the Japs.

THE BOY WHO SLEPT IN CHURCH.

You know the church at Clifton,*
    No doubt you've often been,
And you, perhaps, the ladies
    In oak have likewise seen,
And knights with folded legs, as though
They'd been crusaders long ago.

* Clifton Reynes Church, near Olney, has four oaken effigies of Crusaders and
their wives.

The summer sun was sinking,
  The preacher's voice was deep,
And Willie, not much thinking
  Of sermon, fell asleep,
And very much he was to blame—
Though other boys have done the same.

In vain his mother nudged him
  In vain his sister nipped,
He did not hear the hymn-book
  That to the matting slipped
Between the Fifthly and the next,
And nothing knew of hymn or text.

So shocked were now the ladies
  Of oak with wimples neat
That—pushing off the puppies—
  That slumbered at their feet,
They rose, advanced, and in his ear
Said softly " Do wake up my dear,"

And kissed him. But he woke not
  Though softer on his mouth
Their kisses fell than zephers
  Scent-laden from the south.
At last the knights themselves were forced
To interpose, their legs uncrossed.

And rising, first they righted
  Their helms (both helmets had),
Then clanking down the chancel
  Approached the luckless lad,
They gripped his head, then backward drew,
And bumped it hard against the pew.

At this he screamed " You cowards,
  Touch someone your own size,"
Then straight on him the people,
  And preacher cast their eyes,
And Willie, turning very red
Behind his hymn-book tucked his head.

And after church poor Willie,
  More frightened than a mouse,
Between his frigid parents
  Paced slowly to their house.
His father asked where boys who so
Behave in church expect to go.

His mother breathed more freely
    When nought was said of twig,
His sister found that tiresome boys
    Make convicts when they're big;
Then, sniffing, from a chair she rose
And raised in air her righteous nose.

But Willie, since, has quite reformed—
    No youngster in the town
On Sundays could be more alert—
    He takes the sermon down
In shorthand ; learns, and often quotes,
The text ; and typewrites all his notes.

HE BROUGHT THEM SOMETHING HOME.

A WHALE on business bent, once kissed
    His wife (It is not wrong
To kiss your wife), " Good bye, my dear,
    He said, " I shan't be long."

His child he patted.   As he turned
    Across the main to roam,
They both cried out, " And don't forget
    To bring us something home."

Now as he tunnelled through the deep
    There followed on his track
Six sailors with a big harpoon,
    Who lodged it in his back.

My lordship frowned, as bald men frown
    When flies annoy their pate,
But boat and crew took with him too
    Not having time to wait.

So south for some five hundred miles
    He cleft the briny foam,
And, business done, he turned and made
    For wife and chick at home,

With all the chattels. Then the rope
    Ensnared a raft.   As well
The raft now followed.   Said the whale
    "Another bagatelle ! "

The raft eight babies had on board,
   A mat of wire for wiping
One's shoes, a ladies bicycle,
   And two machines for typing,

A grand piano, several chests
   Of choicest tea from Kandy,
The novels of Sir Walter Scott
   In thirty volumes handy.

An iceberg next among the things
   Got mixed, he never halted,
Joined then a floating tree. Flew all
   The jolter and the jolted.

And when he spied his lintel dear
   His husband's heart dilated,
For wife and chick with loving looks
   Upon his doorstep waited.

Their mouths—some twenty feet across—
   Smiled sweetly through the foam,
And kissing them, " My dears, he said,
   I've brought you something home."
                         3rd Oct. 1896.

THE CRESTED NEWT.

LET him who will to Norway go,
   Or Canada for cod,
And let the salmon lover bear
   To Aberdeen his rod,
But give to me the crested newt,
   To catch him let me go—
The crested newt with spots above
   And orange belts below.

The sturgeon is a royal fish,
   And kingly is the pike,
And those who love them let them take
   As many as they like,
But give to me a certain bank
   A pond, and a worm or so,
And a hungry newt with spots above
   And orange belts below.

And some choose whales—and a big harpoon
    And a mile of rope must fling ;
But what is that to a long thin worm
    And a stick and a yard of string,
And squatting on a spongy bank
    Where flit, and poise, and shoot,
The sapphire needled dragonflies
    That flirt with the crested newt !

And now before his newtly nose,
    The tempting bait you toss ;
With stifled breath, you trembling stand,
    Perspiring like a horse,
You pull, you've got him, how he kicks,
    The hours like minutes go
Sing heigh ! for the pond of crested newts
    With orange belts below.

But those who hanker after whales,
    Or trout, or pike, or cod,
Why let them have their big harpoon,
    Their trowling line and rod ;
But give to me a yard of string
    And a stick and let me go,
To the haunt of the newt with spots above
    And red gold belts below.

THE GLORIOUS WAR.

Suggested by an incident in the Franco-German War of 1870, recorded by Mr.
Archibald Forbes.

I LATELY bought my boy a spade,
    And since it would not do
To show impartiality
    Procured the girl one too,
But since (Regret I've oft expressed)
    They've never let my garden rest.

At last, I said " You two, no more
    Shall dig, you've done enough,"
So shouldering then their implements
    They wandered up the bluff,
And neath a bush of hawthorn flowers
    They drove their spades and dug for hours.

At last they came upon a bone,
  And soon beneath their feet
There lay a long clean skeleton
  With skull and all complete,
Nor were they scared, although the white
And sallow made a gruesome sight.

But when it coolly sat up straight,
  And then assayed to speak,
The girl embraced her brother's arm
  And gave a sudden shriek,
But Fritz said " Hush, be quiet, for
He'll tell about the Glorious War."

Its armbones then it folded
  Upon its cage-like breast,
The sockets where its eyes had been
  It raised, and then addressed
The boy : " My name is Eckenstein,
But what, my little man is thine ?"

" Oh mine is Fritz, and Minna here "—
  " What ! Minna ! did you say ? "—
And loosening then its arms, the thing
  In most attentive way,
Thrust head, then touched her nearest curl,
  " Why Minna was my own dear girl."

" Oh, bother her !" exclaimed the boy,
  " Let's hear about the fight."
"'They can't be separated, sir,
  They're one like frame and kite,
For I and Minna, just before
Were married—in the Glorious War.

" A rose-bud she—a picture
  From coif to dainty shoe—
I see her now—her blushes,
  And low-necked dress of blue,
But ere we kissed—above the hum
Surrounding, came the sound of drum.

" Then Minna turned as pallid
  As these blanched ribs to-day,
I grasped my sword and helmet,
  And pressed her close ; away
Then turned, and left my weeping bride
To join my comrades ranged outside.

" I turned my head to gaze once more,
　When in the room a shell,
Without an instant's warning,
　Upon the table fell.
Flew bridal breakfast, knives, stones, dirt !
But she, thank God, was still unhurt.

"We stood in rank—and yonder slope
　Long lines of Frenchmen streaked—
The chassepots dealt their deadly balls,
　The mitrailleuses shrieked ;
Like hail-stones, when they left the ridge,
The bullets spattered on the bridge.

" And we returned the fire, we reached
　The hawthorn by the moat,
When I was struck, the bullet passed
　Directly through my throat.
I fell : against the tree they found
Me dead, still sitting on the ground.

" In business way, with forty more,
　They shovelled me below,
But anything of Minna
　Besides I do not know—
But what's the broken cross there say?
' Here sleeps—' the rest has dropped away.

" No doubt she raised that mark to me,
　God bless her if she still
Is living—how I loved her !—me
　She loved, and always will "—
" But is that all ? " " That's all." " And so
This happened thirty years ago."

Its bony frame then all collapsed,
　Their spades the children found,
They filled the excavation up,
　And in the lonely mound
They stuck the broken cross piece for
Memorial of the Glorious War.

16th Nov. 1896

HAT SHEP SU.

OR DON'T RUB ANOTHER BOY'S SUMS OUT.

Upon a time, king Thothmes Two
And his vicious sister, Hat Shep Su,
As ancient hieroglyphics show,
O'er Egypt reigned from Noph to No ;
And tablets many Thothmes wrote,
And placed in cities far remote
And cities near at home to tell
How usefully he'd reigned and well—
The towns he took, the men he slew.

But when he died queen Hat Shep Su
Sent out a gang with orders plain
To rub the writings out again.
And they cleaned those tablets small and great
Like schoolboy sums from off a slate,
And in their place (Mean trick to do),
Chiselled the deeds of Hat Shep Su.

But by-and-by the irony
Of fate set up king Thothmes Three,
And Thothmes Three had scarce succceded
When just as she had done so, he did ;
And with a will so earnest that,
Search Egypt through of royal Hat
It's hard to find cartouche or line,
Tablet or hieroglyphic sign.

So, boys, when tempted now, no doubt,
To rub another's cyphering out,
Before that shabby trick you do
You'll bear in mind queen Hat Shep Su.

THE ACID SISTERS.

A Tale of Olney and Clifton Reynes in the time of Edward II.

Canto First.

The Sisters.

I.

Upon the day called Trinity—
Within the undulating sea
    Of buttercup that lies between
The willowed foot of Clifton Hill
And the tapering poplars by the mill
    And church of Olney (dazzling scene !)
Sauntered a lovely maid—none e'er,
One thinks, had face or mind more fair—
A spray of wood-ruff in her hair,
Comporting, each delicious floret,
In modesty with her who wore it.

II.

But every wight in raptures spake,
Within the spacious wapentake,
    Of Amabel, the dainty ward
    Of Roger Somery, the lord
Of Dagnell Manor and Olney Town,
And Culverwell by Yatley Down ;
    So using laudatory strain
We walk within a numerous train.

III.

The night before in Dagnell Court[1]
Sir Roger's guests held gallant sport,
But 'mongst the knights, there glittered none
Like Ralph de Reynes, De Reynes's son

[1] Although Somery owned Olney Castle he is made to live at Dagnell Court. The castles were about this time being deserted as places of residence.

G

From Clifton, whose proud Hall looked down
On cradled, straggling Olney town.
Sir Roger's daughters[1] all were there,
Tall Nichola with tile-red hair,
And Joan, spiteful, squat, and short,
And Anne, acerb, with wen and wart,
And Anastasia, round of back
Like some hunched witch; but for the lack
Of beauty 'twere unkind to scorn them
Had they but manners to adorn them,
But four more disagreeable creatures,
In speech, behaviour, form and features,
You'd hardly find e'en if you sped
From Berwick town to Lizard Head.

IV.

Sir Ralph that night was soon their prey—
" Would I could have my own sweet way ! "
Said he; his longing glances fell
Not once or twice on Amabel.
But no, with Nichola must he pair,
Though he loved not women angulaire,
And next with Joan he trod the floor
Though bending e'er distressed him sore,
Then Anastasia (luckless man !),
Who passed him on to acid Anne;
And when again his glances fell
On blushy, fragrant Amabel
Before a word (he sighed in vain),
With bony Nichola again
He spun, then passed with deep concern
To each of the others again in turn,
Until, arrived at blank despair,
Whether 'twas Anne he did not care,
Or Joan, or gaunt Nichola,
Or bunchy Anastasia ;
He cared not which to him might fall
They were objectionable all.

1 Early in the 14th Century Olney was assigned in equal shares to the four daughters of DeSomery. For their names and characters the author is responsible.

Canto Second.

The Rector.

V.

SWEET Amabel, as through the spray
Of buttercup she held her way,
Mused long upon each incident
Of the notable night, then homeward went;
But scarce had she passed the swinging gate
To thread the alley consecrate
To the juvenile god of the bended bow,
And gazed towards the town, when lo,
The cassock, hood, and figure tall
Appeared above the orchard wall [1]
Of grave Sir John de Buckingham, [2]
The rector; even Tartary's Cham
Was less an autocrat. They met
At the well known spot, where townsfolk yet
Comment, as they point to the twenty chinks,
That the impudent sun at the same time winks
Through every window of the steeple. [3]

VI.

"It likes me not to see my people,"
Exclaimed Sir John, "in field and lea
Upon the day called Trinity;
The soul more nourishment should find
Within yon pile for prayer designed
Than midst this pleasaunce. If you feel
Rebuked, go hasten, maid, and kneel
Before our blessed Lady's shrine,
And pray for your soul's good and mine
And for—"—"But, sir, if flocks should pray,
Should not the pastor lead the way?"
Quoth Amabel, though timorously.
(Canary-coloured fields loved he).
"I would not, sir, presume to search
Your motives, but neither are you at church."

1 "Cherry Orchard." There are no trees now.

2 The Author has allowed himself a little licence with dates. John de Buckingham did not really become Rector of Olney till later—1348.

3 At this spot one can see through all the twenty windows of the steeple.

VII.

Sir John, surprised, his eyebrows raised,
Then in the maiden's visage gazed.
" Sir Ralph de Reynes is dying there,"
And he pointed to the distance, where
Amid thick shrubs and chestnuts tall
Stood out the towers of Clifton Hall.
" Sir Ralph ! " cried Amabel—" I mean
    The father, mouse, and not the son."
The lady blushed. The thrust was keen,
    But well deserved. Exception none,
They fared but ill who hoped in fence
To worst his nimble Reverence.

Canto Third.

In Dagnell Garden.

VIII.

MEANWHILE, fair Dagnell's flowers among,
The sisters talked with venomed tongue
Of Amabel, who, by St. Hugh, they sware
Was the hatefullest creature that breathed God's air.
They flattered themselves they had kept her away
From Ralph on the preceding day,
But voiced the fear that their success
On another occasion might be less.
" I wish," muttered Joan, " the minx would die !"—
" Scorched," added Anne, " with an evil eye,"
And Nichola trusted that on her grave
Nettles might grow—detestible sight !—
Anastasia hoped that every knight
Who mourned her might lose, like her of Sarepta,
A cherished son, or the eye that wept her.

IX.

And as in an arbour with moss o'er run
They seated themselves to avoid the sun,
Said Nichola, " All of you, lend you ears,
I have tried to-day the sieve and shears,
And now not a wisp of a doubt remains
But I, in a year, shall be Lady Reynes."

"Pooh, pooh!" cried Joan, "my palm has been read,
And I am the maid the knight would wed."
"Nay, any unbiassed eye could see,"
Said Anne, "that Sir Ralph doats most on me."—
"What! you, with your warts!" Anastasia said,
"Or Nichola, you! with your firebrand head,
Or you, dwarf Joan! by cock and pie,
Ye lie, fine ladies all, ye lie.
The bride will be me.—Nay, look not black."—
"You," cried the rest, "with your Punch-like back!"
To catalogue all the taunts and jibes
That followed would take a score of scribes,
And from words they had almost come to nails,
When Anne, o'er the tops of the boundary pales,
Descried the head of Amabel.

X.

"Ladies," she cried, "'tis scarcely well
To tilt at the present juncture; see,
In the face of the common enemy;
Resume the melly by and by,
If so you will, but ladies, I,
For one must now abstain." With this
She sealed on Anne's chaste lips a kiss,
And, taking the cue, Anastasia fair
Toyed with Nichola's coarse, red hair,
And Nichola gave a playful slap
To Joan's hard hand upon her lap;

XI.

And when Amabel passed, in dulcet tones,
With endearing terms, they begged for the nonce
That she would come in, but when she declined,
And had left them several yards behind,
They preferred, they said, nor did one disagree,
Her room to her excellent company.

Canto Fourth.

At Clifton Hall.

XII.

MEANTIME, though given up for dead,
De Reynes, the sire, had left his bed;

And John de Buckingham, although
Summoned the last rites to bestow,
Was met upon the castle stairs
By him who had engaged his prayers,
And greeted with a loud guffaw,
Whilst to a menial, " Fellow draw !"
The knight roared out, "and promptly, too,
A flagon of King Edward's brew;
No ale like that within the shire !
King Edward—not the doll, his sire—
Once drank it on this very stair,
And by the Milan blade I wear
The liquor clear that bears his name
To judgment day shall hold the same."

XIII,

They reached the hall whose timbers low
Were graced with spoil of spear and bow.
" Sir Ralph," exclaimed the priest, " my tongue
    Can only feebly tell,
My joy to hear thy lusty lung—
    To see thee hale and well.
Though how so great a change could be
In twenty hours amazes me,
But yesterday you seemed a corse,
To-day you're sprightlier than your horse."

XIV.

" What, cannot you, a priest, divine !
They carried me to Marston shrine
    ' Master John Schorne,
    A gentlemen born,
Conjured the devil out of a boot ';
But you know the rhyme like haunt of coot
And heronshaw," said Sir Ralph with a sly
But perceptible twinkle in his eye.

XV.

" Then I sware," cried Sir John, "you jest or lie ;
You've no more been to Marston spring,
Than my maid Madge to see the king,
And if you had there's nothing truer, you
Infidel, than that it did not cure you,"

XVI.

" Fie, it comes ill from a priest to flout
The saints, and cast on their miracles doubt."—
" 'Tis worse," cried Sir John, " when a belted knight
Inclines 'gainst his lawful king to fight."
The warrior knit his brow and laid
A hand on the haft of his gleamy blade,
But the ale came in, and the sight of it turned
The frown to a smile. " Thou hast fairly earned
A name for speech that bites, but sit,
Sir priest, we freely forgive thy wit ;
You serve a manikin, I a man,
But both can drink of the self-same can."

XVII.

" Sit with a rebel, Sir Ralph, not I."—
" Ha, saucy priest, but you vainly try
To kindle my ire while froths this ale,
Whose graceful aroma suggests the tale
Of our march by Carlisle and Line's winding rill
With Longshanks. Ah ! he was a king if ye will.
I see the gay banners, the armour clad peers,
The long line of archers the forest of spears,
The litter that bore the old king at our head,
'Twas something to follow when such a chief led.
His thin weazen face ! I remember the day
When his worn spirit crept from its cottage of clay—
The gloom in the camp, the rugged cheeks wet,
Whether noble's or yeoman's ; nor can I forget
The shouting that greeted the charge of the dead :
' March forward, and carry my bones at your head !'-
There were visions of battle, and towers toppled down,
Of plunder and loot ; and in Stirling's brave town
In fancy we saw ourselves swaggering. Ah !
But the end of it, Oh, the poor end of it—pah !—
Boy, hurry and fill up the flagon again—

XVIII.

I grant you, once more 'twas strike tent and draw rein,
But on London, not Stirling, our heroes made dash,
Not surtouts, but venison, ambitious to slash.
Instead of Scots' blood, English wine flows apace,
And mail is discarded for satin and lace,

And weblike embroidery, essence and gowns,
And they storm ladies' hearts in the place of Scots' towns,
For pates they crack jokes, and the trumpet's deep bray
Is changed for the tinkling guitar ; by my fay !
'Twas enough to enshroud every true heart with gloom,
And to bring up long Edward again from his tomb.
     But alas, for our land !
     Its prestige has fled,
     Exhausted its sand,
     Our hero is dead,
     The few who would on,
     Are but goats in a tether,
     The Hammer[1] is gone,
     We cringe to a Feather.
But as though to be craven were not enough shame
Our king (save the mark !) further sullies his name
By shameless extortion, and imposts unjust,
To pay for his prodigal courses and lust.
For the base he has gold, for the true a sharp whip,
But he who the wings of the barons would clip
Should be cast in rare mould, and some mettle should show,
But enough of this patter—the varlet is slow
To replenish the flagon—Hi, rascal, make speed !
Who dawdles with liquor he dawdles indeed ! "

XIX.

" Sir Knight," exclaimed the priest, "tis well,
No ear but mine o'erheard this tale.
That words disloyal should be spoken
On such a day as this gives token
Of mind diseased."—"What has occurred
To make men loyal ! Give the word.
Say, have you news ?"—" I have."—" I wot
Our army heads not to the Scot."—
It does."—" Hurrah ! My boy shall don
His new steel suit. With armour on
Among the bravest he shall vie,
God bless thee, priest ! this dimmy eye
Sees bright again. This news has strung
Anew these joints. You see me young.
God bless the king ! Sir priest, I crave
Your pardon.—Ah ! and here's the knave.

1 Edward 1st was called " Hammer of the Scots."

Haply, in my accursed delusion
I might have drunk the king's confusion,
Had he not dawdled. My blessings light
On every dawdler from this night,
No matter what the sex or station,
In what condition, clime or nation :
   Let cannon boom ! blow, varlets, blow !
   Let every trumpet blare !
Rogue Somery in the town below
   Shall hear the blast."—" Forbear,"
Exclaimed the priest. " This should not be
Upon the day called Trinity."

XX.

" The better the day," cried Clifton's lord,
" The better the deed." The crakeys[1] roared
And the trumpets blared, such a terrible din
From brazen throat and culverin
Was never heard on land or sea
Upon the day called Trinity.
The notes rolled far, and high, and wide,
And everyone wondered what might betide.
Rogue Somery swore in Dagnell Court,
There was powder enough to blast a fort.
" Their ways are original, too, up there,
We can die in the town, without the blare
Of trump, and it is not the usual plan
To soothe the ear of a dying man
With culverin throats, to say nought of the waste,
But every gr'hound and hawk to his taste ! "

XXI.

Said Nichola, letting a rouge pot fall,
" Whatever's agog in Clifton Hall ! "—
" Said Joan, applying a brush of dye,
To the brow above her least pleasing eye,
" Sir Ralph must have told his sire that he
Intends, come what may, to marry me."—
" It's much more likely," said contrary Anne,
" That Sir Ralph has explained to the ancient man,
That he doesn't intend such a foolish thing,
And that is the cause of the boom and ding."

---

1 Cannon were just about this time coming into use. The earliest were called crakeys and culverins. They were used in battle in 1327 and possibly earlier,

XXII.

Then next coy Anastasia spoke :
" I dreamt last night of shot and smoke,
  And guns reverberating deep,
    So to me it referred I knew "—
" Invariably when you sleep,"
    Said Anne, " I hear it too,
  But it's odd that in slumber you should hear
  The noise you make yourself, my dear."—
In her chamber on the topmost floor
Of Dagnell, sweet Amabel heard the roar,
And sinking upon her knees she prayed
  That, whatsoe'er the case,
No harm might come (religious maid!)
  To one. In the market-place
Men stood in knots ; on every side
The casement windows opened wide,
And uncombed heads and long-craned necks,
Especially of the softer sex,
Appeared, and many a voice high-pitched
Demanded, like to voice bewitched,
The news. The farm wives thought of thunder,
And feared for the milk, but soon all wonder
Was set at rest, and everyone knew
Why the cannon belched, and the trumpets blew,
And made the assertion, though none could test it,
If they hadn't been told they'd soon have guessed it.

Canto Fifth.

Beware of One !

XXIII.

A FORTNIGHT fled, and in knightly state,
  Sir Ralph the younger sallied down
  From Clifton Hall to Olney town.
He passed the church, and the Rectory gate,
And presently reached the wyverned port,
And entrance hall of Dagnell Court,

A comelier knight, man ne'er did see
Than Ralph de Reynes armed cap-a-pie ;
His bright, frank face and sparkling eye
    Had been the light of his father's hall,
    And ladies marked his figure tall,
And old wives who could prophesy
    By sieve and shears,
    In coming years
By their grandam's grave-rail swore
    That ladies hearts
    He would break like darts,
And that love would breed troubles galore ;
And that he as soldier stout and true
Great deeds of derring-do would do.
    The former half of the prophecy
        Proved true ; the gallant sware
    That of the other moiety ·
        He would himself take care.
A cincture of blue braid was set
Around his blinding bascinet
His hawberk reaching to his knee
Was hid by a chequy surtout. See
His kite-shaped shield
    With a passant rayn [1]
On an argent field,
    All else quite plain ;
His long wide sword in scabbard set,
Gauntlet, and spur and solleret.

XXIV.

" Sir Knight," cried Dagnell's lord, " adieu ! "
    With a hand on Ralph's camail,[2]
" Give good account, whate'er you do,
    Of the foe."—" He cannot fail,"
    Cried Nichola, " o'er hill and dale
Our wishes follow him. Would I might take
A sword and a soldier be ! "—" You'd make,"
Said Anne (aside), " a soldier fair
Were scratching allowed, and pulling hair,
But these, though it's very odd, I'm sure,
Are contrary to the rules of war."

1 The rayn, or deer was the cognisance of the Reynes family.
2 The chain mail covering the neck and shoulders.

"Would I were a fay," said Joan, " with chance
To do as I please, I'd direct your lance,
  Whatever it pointed at, that should yield."—
"Your battle-axe, had I magic," said Anne,
" Should always cleave to the chine its man."
  Said Anastasia, " May your shield
Be true as your Milan sword is keen."
Said Ralph, more solemn than a dean,
  "Kind dames with wit—and—beauty,"
He added courteously, " I mean,
  Please God, to do my duty."

XXV.

Poor Amabel, as each compliment
And good wish flew, had full intent
Herself some pleasant word to say,
But she trembled to think of the coming fray,
And was on the point as they stood below,
  In Somery's pebbled yard,
Of saying she hoped if he struck a foe
  He would not hit him hard :
From bloodshed and strife her heart recoiled,
She strove to say something—but found herself foiled.

XXVI.

But Ralph missed not the lucent tear
  That trembled on her cheek,
And well he marked the lips that moved
  But nathless failed to speak;
So tempting she looked, 'twas in vain to resist her.
So he clasped her sweet form in his strong arms and kissed
  her.
Her mouth it was. She blushed. Likewise
  He blushed, and as a screen
The sisters' hands flew to their eyes
  And hid the shocking scene.
And each, disgusted, tossed her head
  Nor sought to hide a sneer,
And each contemptuously said,
  " Preposterous ! The idea !"

XXVII.

"Cried Ralph, "Good bye, kind dames, good bye,
　And, Somery, adieu!
Of me think now and then, and I
　Will often think of you."
With that he vaulted on his steed,
　The squire renounced the rein,
And through the brilliant yellow mead
　He cantered home again.

XXVIII.

More touching still, the parting here,
　Though warrior scarred and tough,
The sire De Reynes let fall a tear,
　But brushing it off—"Enough
Of folly, and weakness," he said, "Have done!
　A soldier and not calm!
And yet thou art my only son;
　God shield thee, boy, from harm."—
"Do ye fear the Scot will slay me, sir?"—
　"Not so," the father cried—
"Will pestilence be pillager?"
　"No Reynes, boy, ever died
Of plague; we die of age in bed,
　No matter what foeman we face"—
"It possibly, sir," the stripling said,
　"Adumbrates my disgrace,
But be assured, I'll prove no craven."—
"Hark to me, yonder sooty raven
Has three times lit on that wind bent tree,
And three times harshly called to me,
'Beware of one, Oh, beware of one!'
Within my brain they ever run—
Who taught the words I cannot tell,
Their import, yet, I know full well."

XXIX.

"Then 'twas the lady Amabel,"
Cried a dapper page, "when ill you lay
She came to the Cover[1] every day

1 The Fox-Cover.

And sat beneath the wind blown fir,
Where the raven black and sinister
Was wont to perch and wait for her,
And ever in a mournful tone,
' 𝔅𝔢𝔴𝔞𝔯𝔢 𝔬𝔣 𝔬𝔫𝔢, 𝔒𝔥, 𝔟𝔢𝔴𝔞𝔯𝔢 𝔬𝔣 𝔬𝔫𝔢 ! '
She sang, and oft as I passed, I heard
The same refrain and saw the bird."

XXX.

" But of what," said young Reynes, " should I beware
    Save edge of axe, and point of spear ? "—
    " Of the poison cup have constant fear,
Of the very bread you eat take care,
Of even bosom friends beware,
    And most of all suspicious be
    Of foxy Roger Somery ! "

XXXI.

" Of Somery ? You were hand and glove,
Ten days ago.   Was so much love
But wind and bladder ? "—"Do not linger,"
Exclaimed the sire, the whiles his finger
Pointed adown the avenue,
Where now full clearly stood in view
A group of horse. " Whate'er will be
    If life to me remains,
From his own gallows Somery,
    Shall dangle in his chains."
The father and the son embraced,
" Adieu, adieu," he cried in haste.
A moment his strong arms entwine
The dainty form of Rosmarine[1]
    His lovely and beloved sister ;
" Dew of the sea, God shelter you,"
To horse he sprang, but waved adieu
    Again far down the vista.

1 Rosmarine, (rhymes sign, etc.,) means " Dew of the Sea," or " Sea Spray."

Canto Sixth.

The Benediction in Olney Church.

XXXII.

THE group within the avenue
    Comprised the youth and chivalry
    Of those fraternal Hundreds Three
That Ouse meanders through :
Bonstow from Bonstye[1] called, whose sun
    Sank low when Newport's star
Arose ; Molestow[2] from Emberton
    Southward extending far ;
And Sigelai, whose fat lands none
    Surpassed, triangular.
Amongst that gallant company
Full many a soldier might ye see
Of proud and ancient family
For prowess famed in fray:
    Swart Aylesbury, De Blossomville,
    Ralph Pipard and De Longueville,
Barre, Caron and De Grey ;
The Huntes from Walnut land,[3] the three
Tall Chesters from sweet Chicheley,
    And Ivo Loughton suave,
Sir Roger Tyringham, and Lane,
Vache, Sherrington, and Peter Mayne,
    And Filiol rash and brave,
Sir Robert Olney rich and vain,
Whose sire at Weston raised the fane
    The Olneys slept and sat-in—
St. Lawrence Church, where you may see
The brass unto his memory
    With eulogy in Latin.

---

1 The vanished town of Bonstye stood near Gayhurst. Its inhabitants removed
to Newport Pagnell.
2 The Hundreds of Newport were Bonstow, Molestow and Sigelai.
3 Walton is famed for its walnuts.

XXXIII.

There was Peyvre, too, from Laundon[1] keep,
John Cauz, and Harry Fountain,
And Fremband from Bow Brickhill steep—
Newportia's only mountain—
That Fremband who, a pard in fray,
Was deep as any sea
In love, yet not a word dare say
Through his timidity,
Though he oft would sigh, " Dear lady mine,
Fair Rosmarine, sweet Rosmarine ! "

XXXIV.

Lo many, too, of less degree,
A goodly gallant company.
Now wend they all their devious course
Adown the hill, the mead across
That Amabel had trod,
Anxious in Olney's steepled fane
Their expedition great might gain
The benison of God.

XXXV.

Dismount they at the churchyard gate,
The menials with their horses wait,
The knights the church drew near,
Like silver plaques their basnets shone,
Flamed surtout, shield, and gonfalon
Flashed battle-axe and spear.
Entering, they thread the nave in rank,
The fabric echoes to the clank
And rattling voice of steel.
The priests door opens, entering, see,
The choirmen—numerous company—
And priests in long procession file
Rich vestmented within the pile,
And last of all there sped,
Splendid in fringy alb and scroll,—
Embroidered chasuble, and stole,
De Buckingham their head.

1 Old name for Lavendon. It is so called in the ancient registers.

XXXVI.

The warriors knelt, and ne'er, I ween,
Was viewed a more impressive scene
   Within that chancel wide.
Martyr and saint in splendid hue
Of carmine, yellow, green, and blue
   Looked down; the Crucified
Upon the rood screen's tracery rich[1]
Hung crówned with thorns; in Gothic niche
Becanopied St. Paul one sees,
And holy Peter with his keys.
   The walls are frescoed o'er, and in
Cinereous tints depict the end
Awaiting those who madly spend
   Life's precious hours in shameful sin ;
While in compartments higher
   Winged seraphs beatific,
Mid psaltery and lyre,
   And trump and hieroglyphic,
Conduct o'er causeways asper[2]
To halls of gold and jasper
Who unto good aspire.

XXXVII.

But to describe minutely here
Each storied wall and window pane
Might tire. Within the glorious fane
The mass proceeds, the litany,
   The service draws to close,
Pronounced the Benedicite,
   The maily warriors rose
To quit the holy house. Again
The clank of armour haunts the fane.

XXXVIII.

Arrived beyond the churchyard gate,
They mount again—the townsfolk wait
To see the bustling, gallant show,
By Warwick Yard[3] and Arms they go,
And Dagnell wall where wall-flowers blow,

1 Olney Church was formally splendidly decorated. The rood screen was destroyed early in the present century.
2 Rough. The way to heaven is asper and painful.—Sir T. More.
3 The Author's own house and garden were formally called Warwick Yard.

H

And as they passed—not strange to tell—
Sir Ralph bethought of Amabel ;
Then through the broad High Street they ride,
With willows down the western side,
And a streamlet on whose mimic tide
Serenely sailed a whole flotilla
Of ducks more white than Olney's miller.
Then young and old from byre of cow,
And osier shed, and sty of sow,
   From forge and high pitched roofs
Flock out; arises high the din,
Men's voices rough and women's thin,
Whilst hat and kerchief wave ; chime in
The urchins rash who risk their skin
   Against the horses' hoofs.

XXXIX.

For Olney dearly loves to see
Procession fair and pageantry,
Whether of squadrons bound for war,
Or squires equipped to hunt the boar,
Processions priestly, funeral, or
The flower-bescattered bridal ; for
Engendered 'neath a prying star
   They have peculiar itch
For sights, so only sights they are,
Imposing or triobolar,
   It matters little which.
They pass the castle's gloomy sides,
   The pond [1] where Somery's fish are stored,
   The gallows[2] grim of Olney's lord
Where next the road divides,
And on its arm the carcase hung
Of one who let a wagging tongue
Revile De Somery's steward strong.
His fate was not uncertain long ;
For Salcote gave him to the chains,
And from his putrefied remains
At their approach there gabbling rose
A flock of loathsome daws and crows.

---

1 Now called the Whirly-pits.
2 At the junction of the Warrington and Lavendon roads.

Canto Seventh.

The Battle.

XL.

KING Edward's host, all England's pride,
Was camped old Tweed's swift stream beside,
   Whose waves through Berwick wind—
Berwick that oft its masters changed,
Now Scotch, and now with England ranged,
   To siege and raid resigned ;
Where, victim to King Edward's rage,
Fair Lady Buchan in a cage
   Of wicker years had pined.
Within that host no heart more light
Than Reynes's ; eager for the fight
   He chafed at each delay.
Ambitious to obtain renown,
He grudged beside the border town
   Each wasted hour and day.

XLI.

Renown ! strange food ! yet wherefore sit
   To judge the soul who on it feeds,
In every age your man of grit
   For love thereof has done great deeds.
The fetters forged by tyrant sloth,
   Which perfectly our bodies fit,
Ambition can unclasp—can both
   Divide the links and manumit
The wretched slave ; unto His name
   Be praise, who put elation
Within men's hearts at thought of fame
   And human approbation.
Yet better not to feel thy prod,
   Ambition, than that we
Should misapply that gift of God,
   Incessant energy—
A platitude, I grant you, yet
A platitude we oft forget,
Therefore 'tis but a venial sin
To rub it vigorously in.

XLII.

This journey to the land of heather
One disapproves of altogether,
Oh, why could they not leave alone
The Scots, and Bruce upon his throne,
We hold the campaign was not needed,
But as for Ralph, 'tis certain he did.
So 'tis a waste of time to wrangle,
And on the pros and cons to jangle,
For no man, if so be he fights,
Marries, or vegetates, or writes,
Can act superior to his lights.

XLIII.

But hark ! what thunderous shout is sent
Into the azure firmament !
When Edward struck his royal tent
And " Forward!" was the word they sped
To northward.   Three broad shires they thread,
And league on league the army spread,
Like fabulous sea monster dread,
The denizen of ocean's bed,
Whom seamen yearly from the dead
For our diversion raise,
With zeal outstripping praise,
When times are dull, and work is slack,
And news sheets suffer much from lack
Of copy.   Stand they face to face—
The Scotchmen and the English race—
Forests of bowmen, halberdiers,
And lakes of bascinets and spears,
Like silver bright, and banners gay,
Strong horse and foot in proud array :
The battle's joined, tremendous sight !
Two sturdy nations locked in fight !

XLIV.

O Bannockburn ! can England bear
To hear thy name pronounced ? but where
Can nation proud be found whose story
Records no dire reverses gory!

Prussia had Jena; France has known Sedan;
And Russian annals tell of Inkermann;
To Scotland Flodden Field was dealt;
At Austerlitz the Austrians felt
The bitterness of overthrow:
Doth Italy Adowa know!
At Cannae came to Rome the turn;
And England had her Bannockburn.

XLV.

The arrows fly; the cavalry
Of Scotland charge; our archers flee,
Sweep sword and crushing axe;
Our English horse dash bravely on,
Flash sword and spear, gleams gonfalon!
(No courage England lacks)—
Only to fall in trap and pit,
Devised by keener Scottish wit.
The frightened steeds their riders threw,
The Scots had but to pour and slay,
'Twas not, that John the Baptist's day,
A fight but a battue.
In Africa the wild Zulu
Delights with fellow braves to make
A ring enormous, lessen it,
Thus drive into a central pit
The desert herds from veldt and brake.
Then, as the creatures romp and gore
Each other, on their flanks they pour
A hail of pointed assegai,
And so, till tired of slaying, slay.
'Twas such a scene in Scotland then,
Excepting that for beasts put men.
But still by stalwart captains led
The English host preserved the fight,
When down from rugged Gillies' height
A second host appeared in sight,
Or so it seemed, with banners bright—
An apparition dread;
Despair succeeded, flagged the fray,
And England's baffled worn array
With ignominy fled,

Canto Eighth.

The Hermit of Hermit's Tongue.

XLVI.

Now turn we from that gory plain
To Clifton's pleasant fields again ;
The bridle path to Clifton Hill
Was badly worn, 'tis rugged still—
Not mauled by heel of village youth,
But by the keen erosive tooth
Of Father Ouse who oft forsakes
In winter time his bed, and makes
At will far-stretching seas and lakes.
Nay, sometimes, on a summer's day
His dripping arms lift high the hay
And bear it off with quiet glee
Towards the distant German sea.
Beyond the stream the pilgrim may,
If willing, take the narrow way
That leads him past the clacking mill[1]
And onward up the thymy hill ;
Or if to rove he be inclined
In aimless mood, with vacant mind,
To fish, make love, or meditate,
He'll turn him, having passed the gate,
And saunter idly down a tongue
Of land, high grass and reeds among,
And feathery reed-stalks curious,
And cranesbill blooms purpureous,
Where those whom ladies' love makes bold
May fill their arms with iris gold—
Called " Moses in the bulrushes."
By toddlers small who pull rushes
And turn them—nimble-fingered schemers—
To boats and ivory funnelled steamers.
At yonder stand of roughly ripped
Uneven planks the flocks are dipped,
Then turned within a hurdled pen
To wait the dexterous shearing men,

1 Now disappeared.

Their bleatings mingling with the notes
From thrush and glorious blackbird throats.
(Think of it, ye in dingy attic
Mid smoky London's roar and racket!)

XLVII.

Some forty paces from this stand
Within the enchanting Tongue of land
Stood a symmetric hawthorn tree
Which in Mid-May when May flowers blow
Seemed a gargantuan ball of snow,
And later was in mantle dressed
More scarlet than a robin's breast.
Beneath this tree, the passer by
Upon the bridge a glimpse would catch
Of rough warped door, stone walls, and thatch ;
And, curious, drawing nigh,
　　Would come upon a hut, and see
A bearded man more thin than sheeted
Ghost upon the threshold seated—
　　A book upon his knee.
But ever at his hermitage
He pours upon the written page,
　　The passer by he nothing heeds,
He does not even raise his head,
He hears no syllable that's said,
　　He only reads, and reads, and reads.
At dusk, secured the clasp's brass hook,
He puts aside his precious book,
　　And tells his Bethlehem beads.
At night within his hovel bare
He lies upon a pallet spare—
　　No bar upon his door :
For simple would that robber be
Who looked to find a treasury
　　Within a hut so poor.
　　Ascetics need not bars and locks,
Yclad in scapular. circingle,
Cowl, and hair-shirt, beside a dingle,
　　The lair of wolf, and fox,
And badger.　Here for years he'd dwelt,
This hermit ; on his leathern belt

Was written, wording else was none,
Beware of one, Oh, beware of one !
The very enigma curiously
Of the raven on the wind blown tree,
But there is many a mystery
    Beneath the ancient sun.

XLVIII.

Mild penance, verily, it were
To hob-a-nob with the hermit spare
    In summer blithe and bright,
Fenced in by flag and butomus,
With larks by day to sing to us,
    And nightingales at night ;
But when the trees are black and bare,
And Boreas plays his antics there,
    When boughs with snow
    And sleet hang low,
And Ouse's fickle waters rise
With lap and plash 'neath ashy skies
Until they soak the hermit's floor,
And cataracts down the chimney pour,
And none can from the hovel stir
Except by boat, I might prefer,
(Though charming the romantic shed),
A sounder roof and drier bed.

Canto Ninth.

Limping Hugh the Leper.

XLIX.

Three months had passed since Ralph had said
Adieu and northerly had sped,
When crossed there Olney market-hill—
Oft in my dreams I see him still—
A form that limped yet almost ran,
It was—nay it was not—a man,
But what a man had one time been ;
His left hand held a bowl of treen,
The right a bell, a bottle brown
Of leather from his waist hung down,
His very name confusion spread,
The children left their games and fled,

Like leverets startled in a wood.
His head was covered with a hood,
His face was veiled from sight likewise,
But glittered his unhealthy eyes
Through two round holes ; his gabardine
Of coarse, loose stuff was old and mean,
And ever as his footsteps fell
He rang his melancholy bell.

L.

It was the leper, Limping Hugh,
Well-known the Newport Hundreds through.
From town to town his figure thin
Went halting.   At the thought of him
Curdled the blood.   Though timorous, yet
The folk their doles did not forget,
But on the smooth, great step-stone, set
Convenient for mounting horse,
Hard by the central Market Cross,[1]
They laid such scraps of food that their
Not over burdened shelves could spare,
And having placed their liberal dole
Retired.   The leper filled his bowl.
'Mong those who to the horse-stone stole
Was Amabel ; a loaf of bread
She laid upon the stone and fled.

LI.

But ere the leper filled his treen
Enacted was a startling scene
    In Roger Somery's hall :
Upon a bench in hunting gear
Sat Somery, a long, stout spear
    Between him and the wall.
Beside, his creature Salcote stood,
A hunting knife with haft of wood
    Within his leathern belt.
Before them on the rush strewn floor
A wretched man besprinkled o'er
    With flour, a-tremble knelt.
" Forgive, my lord, Oh, let me live !"—
" Rapscallion, how can I forgive

[1] Olney Market Cross has disappeared.

Ere thou thy crime unroll,
But speak, for by John Schorne I swear,
I will not hurt a single hair
    Upon thy wretched poll."—
" Then listen, sire, I baked my bread,
And by request I stamped a sign
Upon one loaf, and, bound in twine,
Unto it did I then commit
A letter, which it seems was writ
To Ralph de Reynes, and, brief to tell,
The loaf to Lady Amabel
I gave—her who commissioned me
To do the deed."—Quoth Somery,
With stifled rage: " Is't Reynes you name ? "—
" It was," exclaimed the churl, the same !
The lady's husband."—" Husband, hound ! "
A death-like stillness reigned around.
The menials gazed upon the ground,
And scarcely dared the myrmidan-
In-chief aslant that face to scan,
So terrible in wrath.   A hound
Whined feebly and the eldritch sound
Unto the marrow sent a shiver.   ,

LII.

It were a god-send to deliver
From such a tension if one durst.
At last the pent up tempest burst.
So terribly outpoured the tide
Of ire that in it had he died
Not one, I wot, had shown surprise.
His lips, his cheeks, his dagger eyes
Mirrored the furnace vividly.
" It cannot, shall not, must not be !
By Heaven !" he burst tumultuously,
And word and oath in torrent dread
Tripped up each others heels.   " And wed !
Who wedded them, the dog shall rue it
His false life through ? "   " I didn't do it,"
The baker whined.   A hearty kick
Rewarded him.   " Rapscallion, quick,
The name!"   The wretched helot flung
    A look of supplication up,
" It was the monk of Hermit's Tongue."

LIII.

O'erbrimmed with this Sir Roger's cup,
And in his frenzy blind he swore
More passionately than before.
On baker, Ralph, and Amabel,
Impartially his curses fell,
And the monk, but all monks, he raved, were a parcel
Of knaves, whom the dungeon of Olney Castle
Would purely suit, and that very minute,
If he had a score he would thrust them in it.
" Fetch me the loaf ?" (Just then a page
Unnoticed slipped out—a stripling sage);
" The lady, alas ! that my words are true,
Bestowed it to-day on Limping Hugh."—
" Haste, Mayne!" cried Somery, " Ellis go ;
After him with thy surest bow,
If he escape of my wrath have fear,
And slay him like a boar or deer.
You, Scarlet Fetlock, fetch the shears,
Crop close to his head this rascal's ears,"—
" Mercy ! you promised "—" You hear what I say !
Hurry the yelping rogue away !
Had I but another to bake my bread,
Instead of his ears, it had been his head—

LIV.

Yet stay—'tis a weakness most absurd—
But, just for this once. I will keep my word.
Haste, square-cap, in the wake of me,
And if sport's to be seen, that sport we'll see—
Yet, first unto the dovecote[1] go
And fetch, you long-legged Wellbelow,
The lady Amabel.   I hear
She's feeding the pigeons somewhere near,
And bid her in her bower to stay
Till my return.   And now, away ! "

LV.

Down Olney street old Somery strode,
And made him for the Yardley Road,

---

1 The dovecote of Dagnell Manor, a square building, the lower portion of which
was used as a stable, has only recently been demolished.

The baker following in his white
Square-cap, and sleeves, ceruse with fright.
Meantime the obedient archers drew
The luckless limping leper to,
And like a dog they shot him through.
Six paces from his corpse they stayed
In doubt how next to act. Afraid
To gather nearer—(Better touch a Jew !)
When, suddenly, De Somery's bugle blew,
So, though in dread of being rated,
For their high lord's approach they waited.

LVI.

Hard by, the slant hill's highest ground
Was by a lofty beacon crowned
    Made up of oak-lap sinuous,
Like to a heap of tangled snakes
So wreathed that from default of breaks
    The creatures seem continuous.
Below, inspection keen might see
    Some thinner wood and drier.—
Ignited, all would instantly
    Leap up to warning fire.

LVII.

Quickly, in shorter time indeed
Than priest could rattle through a creed,
The knight got up, but the baker, who
Pretended that within his shoe
A thorn had got, proceeded slowly,
Although the knight gesticulated,
And never for a breath abated
His flow of classic words and holy,
Until the luckless baker gained
The spot, which he at last attained,
And so completed the quartette.

LVIII.

" Now knave unto the corpse, and get,"
    Said Somery, "the packet neat
By you inserted in the bread."
    The baker, whiter than a sheet,
Dropped on his knees, and quaking said,

Or stammered: " My lord, 'tis leprosy,
And one with it fell last Hallowe'en
Who only touched his gabardine,
   Have, pity, oh my lord, on me !"
" I tell thee, once more, fellow, go,
Ellis, again distend thy bow.—
Now, coistril, forward, cap to shoe
Search yonder corpse or you're one too,
An arrow or so your midriff through,"
It was a painful sight to see
The wretched creature tremblingly
Take step—A-suddenly he stopped,
Swooned like a tender girl and dropped.

LIX.

Now, as it chanced, hard by, a cock
   Of twitch burnt bright, and watching it,
   Though several hours it had been lit,
Stood a poor ploughman in a smock,
His big hands, rough, and foul, and coarse,
   As were the garments that he wore,
   An oatbag and a halter bore,
Designed, no doubt, to catch by force
Combined with craft some wily horse.
The scene suggested to the knight
   Ideas soon put in practice ; for
" Go Mayne," he cried, " to yonder wight,
   His halter shall this body draw
   Unto the beacon ; in the straw
And wood we'll burn it, then there'll be
An end to loaf, letter, and leprosy."
The knight's commands were put in force,
Towards the pile they drag the corse,
And in less time than we could name
Both corpse and pile were wrapped in flame.

Canto Tenth.

The Siege of Olney Church.

LX.

In Olney the folk with great amaze
Saw the curling smoke and the ruddy blaze.

Some thought the Scots were nigh at hand,
    And some that the Welsh were giving trouble,
And some that a wild marauding band
    Meant mischief under Robin Double—
A robber chieftain whom the knight
Desired to trap (they wished he might,
And with him catch likewise his train ;
So that no more this smiling plain
The rogues would harry, or combine
To carry off sheep, cows, and swine.)
So some snatched pitchfork, spear, or sword,
And some for knife or bludgeon roared,
And some until they shone like new
Furbished their shields.   Churl, artisan,
And bowman to the High Cross ran.
The swineherd left his pigs and sow,
The cowherd left his half milked cow,
The barber scalpel, brush and strop,
The blacksmith let his bellows stop,
The nimble cobbler dropped his shoe,
The scrivener from his sandbox flew,
The jolly butcher armed with knife,
Cleaver, and steel, to his jollier wife
Bid quick adieu, the tailor shed
His snippits, scissors, tape, and thread,
Mine host of the " Bull " his leather bottle
Forsook, the fletcher his hut of wattle,
And half made arrow—shaft and feather :
Thus flocked they one and all together
Unto the cross, and there they waited.
Such motley crew ne'er congregated
To fight *pro aris et pro focis**
Or hardly ever, one supposes.
For arms, scythe, sickle, bill and crook,
No very military look
Did they present, in jerkin dun,
    Smock frock, and leather apron old,
And some with hats, and some with none.
    It matters not ; their hearts were bold,
And if your heart is brave and true
It matters not what kind of shoe
You wear, or whether to your back
A coat you have or coat you lack.

* For altars and hearths.

LXI.

There soon ensued mid boor and boor
   Discussion animated,
And each of other asked wherefore
   They met, and why they waited.
But none could anything declare
Except he'd seen the smoke and flare.
But soon adown the street there strode
   De Somery and his henchmen twain
   Young Ellis and tall Peter Mayne,
While opposite, post haste, there rode
As if returned from church or ford
Young Wellbelow, who hailed his lord.
Cried Somery : "Quick ! thy business say,
Hast done it, quickly yea or nay ? "—
"I hasted to the cote," he said,
"But Lady Amabel had fled,
It seems your page slipped out and told
   The scene enacted in your hall ;
The boy—and noble sire, in truth,
A perter, slyer, nimbler youth,
I never saw, and in a hurry
I hardly shall—most boys cause worry."—
"Would every boy," said Somery,
"Were at the bottom of the sea.

LXII.

Go on."—"Straight to the church they sped,
   And by the great high altar she
   In fear has taken sanctuary,
And Buckingham hath trumpeted
That he with candle, book, and bell,
   (The gift of pious Hugh of Chester),
   On any daring to molest her
Will hurl the Church's curse. As well
The priest to the teeth has armed his ten
Big brawny-chested serving men."—
"By women, shall I flouted be,
And boys and priests !" cried Somery.
"What can the haughty churchman ail,
   Of me he has seen enough to know
That hectoring will nought avail,
   That I can give two blows for blow,

But priests, the lessons that you set them,
Take long to learn, and soon forget them.
Still, whatsoever motives urge him,
Upon me be the task to scourge him.
Thinks he that his curse to me brings fears,
I'll burn his church about his ears."
By now had come the body guard
Of twenty yeomen from the yard
Of Dagnell armed with six foot bow,
And yard long shafts.   Young Wellbelow
    Their leader was.   Ten more in steel
With axe and spear led Peter Mayne.

LXIII.

The churchyard soon the party gain
    With half the parish at their heel.
Towards the West Door, Somery strode.
    Five paces in front De Buckingham stood
    In cassock, circingle, and hood,   .
And against his foemen barred the road.
Behind, with their backs against the wall,
Stood Buckingham's servants stout and tall,
Five with bow and arrow white,
Five with axe in armour dight.
" Your errand, Roger Somery,
Why come ye arméd thus to me ? "

LXIV.

Said Somery, " You know full well,
Restore me Lady Amabel."—
" Think you that I'm a Bachingdenn,[1]
A girl, a coistril, or a wren !
I blankly, sire," the churchman said,
" Refuse."—" Thy blood be on thy head."
Cried Somery.   " Men assail the door ! "—
Cried Buckingham, " Good swordsmen draw,
And bowmen bend your bows ; surcease
Ye Dagnell men, and give us peace.
Why on ye will ye draw the rod
Of Heaven, and slay the priest of God !

---

1 Nicholas de Bachingdenn a former Rector of Olney had been bullied by the Countess of Arundel, and robbed of his horses, cows, and other live stock.

Here stand I, John de Buckingham,
To balk the wolf, to shield the lamb.
Who thinks to thread this portal wide
Must first my lifeless body stride.
Ye bowmen mine, lay down your bows,
Sheath swords.   Alone I face my foes."

LXV.

And as he spoke upon him came
A light as of seraphic flame,
O God! it is a noble sight
To see a man stand up for right!
Could our dim eyes but pierce through space,
Could we the mist and haze displace,
Methinks we should afar descry
Over the battlemented sky,
With faces downward turned, a crowd
Of blessed witnesses endowed
With joy and expectation blent,
And see them wave encouragement.
But if a holy nimbus came
Upon the priest, suffused with shame
The faces ignorant and rude
Of the opposing multitude.
And though De Somery again
Cried " Forward," did each man refrain.

LXVI.

Forward alone he rushed, his raised
Keen Milan in the sunshine blazed,
When suddenly a sound arose
Of falling glass and vigorous blows.
De Somery dropped his sword ; and jibe
Succeeded threat and diatribe.
" No need to go as far as that
And spit you like a capon fat—
Nor would I have been long about it—
But, hark, the deed is done without it.
My men now tread the chancel floor—
What matter window-light or door,
So long as soldiers gain their ends
And sweet reward their craft attends !"—

I

" If, sire, you think that Amabel
Is in your power, then let me tell
That more than half an hour ago
She left the church.   I think you know
In the churchyard wall a little door
'Neath a cherub's head.   You set great store
Upon your wit ; for me, I meant
Your knavery to circumvent.
We've gained a little time, no doubt,
Ah, wherefore do the people shout ? "

LXVII.

For, lo, the heaving mob divides,
And through, a Benedictine rides.
Dismounting, soon Sir John he spies.
The friends each other recognise.
" Sir John, I've made the maddest burst
To bring the news myself the first,
(Why holds this man a naked sword ?)
My friend, I greet you first, my lord
Of London."—" Hark to that ! Sir John
Is made a bishop," cried a churl.
In the air a hundred rough hats whirl,
And twice a hundred honest throats
Roar out hurrahs ; the tumult floats
Above the sea of honest people,
And scares the jackdaws in the steeple,
Who much commenting on the sound
Above the churchyard circled round.
Sir John a sign for silence made,
Then dropped upon his knees and prayed.

LXVIII.

De Somery, doubtful what to do,
At length from out the churchyard drew,
For ne'er did prayer and homily
With his weak stomach yet agree.
Besides he'd sworn by Marston well
To find out Lady Amabel.
That in the fane she did not hide
He now was truly satisfied,
For all in vain had been the search
In every cranny of the church,

And trusting to mature reflection
He thought he'd hit on the direction
She'd travelled in, therefore,
  Homeward then sped the warrior bold
  That he might consultation hold
With his sweet daughters four.

LXIX.

" My loves," said he, " it irks me much
  That I hot words should say,
But matters had arrived at such
A pass—Alack-a-day!
For Amabel...."—"That she would do
Some mischief, sire, I always knew,"
Said Nichola, " and now its true."
Said Joan, " She hath not crossed me thrice
For nought : toad, serpent, cockatrice,
And every other toothy thing
With talon, poison, beak, or sting !"
Said Anastasia, " Joan, dear,
I had a singing in my ear
This morning, and dame Stowe explains
It augurs ill to Ralph de Reynes."—
" May the sign come true," said Joan, " and may
He fall in battle this very day."—
" If he cross a stream, may he sink and drown,"
Said Anne, " or may someone hold him down,
May he lie like a log in the river bed,
And, when greedy pike on his flesh have fed,
In the naked sockets of his eyes
May crayfish crawl, and eels likewise."—

LXX.

" A truce to your spite," De Somery said,
" And tell me whither is Amabel fled !
Shall we find, my dearest loves," said he,
" The quarry in Harrold Nunnery ?"—
" Nay, nay," they cried, in voices shrill,
" You would find her, rather, at Bow Brickhill."—
" To Bow Brickhill," said he, " you may go,
And take, if you will, young Wellbelow.
But I, and Mayne shall go with me,
Will gallop to Harrold Nunnery."

Canto Eleventh.

The Assassin.

LXXI.

MEANWHILE away in the north countree,
De Reynes, a weary refugee,
Was working southward. From the foe
Small harm he got, as battles go.
He lost a finger, but gained, instead,
In the flesh of his side an arrow head,
And in grievous pain he tramped about
Till a mendicant barber cut it out.
As he threw himself down one weary night
A week or two after the fatal fight,
His thoughts went home, as they'd been perforce
So often, to dear old Olney cross.
And he pictured it, socket, shaft, and pinnacle,
And Amabel by; no need of adminicle
To bring, e'en in that forbidding place—
A hole in a rock—her beauteous face.

LXXII.

Then kindly sleep upon him stole,
And he dreamt in that far off darksome hole,
Of Ouse's waters, limpid, bright,
And lilies immaculately white,
Its meadows, and willows, and arrowheads,
And forget-me-nots and osier beds—
The scenes that with Amabel he'd trod,
And he thought he was there with her—O God!
For, when he bent him down to kiss her, she
    Demurred, and would, on no account, permit him,
    Then, like a wild cat, up she sprang and bit him;
The warm blood trickled. "Miserable me!"
He cried. The vision vanished; in its place
A comrade ran (no dream), he gave him chase,
But loss of blood prevented further stir.
He recognised the would-be murderer

As one he had befriended often, man
To Salcote, rogue De Somery's myrmidon.
Then to his mind the warning came;
" Upon me resteth grievous blame ! "
Said he, " I shall be yet undone ! "
' Beware of one, Oh, beware of one ! '
That he, henceforth, never might forget
He fixed on his wrist an amulet
With Persian characters. At York he lay
Down with a fever, thought to die each day,
And a rascally leech in Somery's pay
Took most of his little blood left away,
And tried to force on him a nauseous drench
As he tossed, distraught, on his bed-called bench,
But in spite of his shocking privations, at length
He recovered his former high spirits and strength :
And the very first chance—stirred well with his sword—
    He made the concoction much thicker,
And, under compulsion, the wretched leech poured
    Down his own throat the horrible liquor.
And to judge by the faces he made as he swallowed it,
'Twould scarce have been worse if the bottle had followed
    it.

LXXIII.

Then south the craven hound and he
Together trudged in company.
To a tavern at Leicester near they drew,
    No sack would Ralph put to his lip,
    Until the leech had first ta'en sip,
For capon and bread he was taster, too,
At Harb'rough the rogue was left for dead,
His fate by both attributed,
To a cantle of cheese supplied that day
By mine host of " The Loaded Wagon of Hay,"
Who like every one else seemed in Somery's pay.
" Henceforth," said Reynes, " I will not eat
Of anything save of unground wheat,
    That morsel, I see,
    Was meant for me.
Yet, sometimes, his plain fare to vary,
He added to his dietary.

Such luxuries as " good fat hen,"*
With " way-bread," * added now and then ;
And little in kickshaws, too, he spent
For " sauce alone "* was his condiment.
And liquor none to his lip would bring
Save that just limbecked from the spring—
A resolution those with poppy
Proboscises might wisely copy.
" The which," said he, " is wisely done,
For I, 'tis clear, must Beware of one !"
And then he loudly and blithely sang,
And the hills with his lusty carol rang ;
For your man of war is always gay,
And his troubles fade like mists away,
When a mouthful he gets of his native air,
And he knows there's waiting for him a pair
Of quite indescribable, melting lips,
And a bosom warm.   He lightly trips—
De Reynes—and he hugged himself, as yet
He had not been caught in Somery's net,
And he looked to the day when from home he should fare
   At the head of a gallant company,
   And chastise for his villany
The badger in his castle lair.

LXXIV.

To Amabel his thoughts now roam
But, nearly there, is not quite home,
And the old saw says that nobody should
Whistle until they're out of the wood.
When you think, says a Book that is read by all,
You stand, you're pretty sure to fall.
And so experienced Ralph de Reynes ;
   In the morning free as carolling lark
At night he sat in filth and chains
   In Somery's Olney dungeon dark
The crafty old spider, with wicked old eye,
Balked oft, had caught at the last his fly.

* Names of herbs.

Canto Twelfth.

At Bow Brickhill.

LXXV.

MEANWHILE sweet, hunted Amabel,
Escaped from the church, had reached the cell
Upon the leafy Tongue, and told
Her troubles to the hermit old.
But as she spoke an adjoining heap
  Of leaves and reeds rose up ; she saw
A man from out their covering creep—
  Alarmed, she darted to the door.
" Fear nought," a loud voice cried, and deep,
  " It's only Nicholas home from war.
Afraid, dear cousin ? And wherefore ? "
She turned. Before her stood the form
Of Fremband. " Oh, my cousin, tell,
Cried palpitating Amabel,
" If Ralph, my Ralph's alive and well !"—
" Ah, ah ! all lovers under the sun,
Are alike," said he, " ye would hear of one,
The one ye happen to love best.
Satisfied, cousin ; your minds would rest
Were half the pride of England lost,
Yes, he is well, but oh the cost
To England of that fatal fray !
Of all that gallant brave array
Who on that balmy summer day
Waited in Clifton avenue,
And unto yonder steeple drew,
To crave Heaven's blessing—Misery !
Returns but one ; and wretched he ;
But fortune never smiled on me,
Oh would, dear cousin, I were dead,
A good Scot's claymore through my head.
Ah woe is me ! by sorrow led,
I sought for death it would not come,
But wherefore should I ever strum
This mournful string."—" Your misery,"
Said Amabel, " doth torture me,
For none would I in trouble see.
Prithee your tale of woe rehearse,"

LXXVI.

"I love the lady Rosmarine,
Oh would," said he, "that she were mine,
But on my head there rests a curse,
I cannot, cannot live," said he,
"Or die, Oh miserable me!"—
"But why, why wretched ?"—"Children," cried
The hermit, "stem ye both the tide,
Of talk; this lady needs must ride
To Brickhill—to thy father's; say
Wilt thou conduct her, yea or nay ?
Thou wilt. Then yonder in the Leys*
A pair of tethered horses graze,
The time admits of no delay,
God shield you, lady, now away."

LXXVII.

In silence all the course they ride,
Between their steeds a distance wide.
Petsoe and Ekeney they thread,
By Emberton's tree and cross[1] they sped;
St. Laud's[2] proud fane they leave behind,
Up Newport's steepy street they wind,
Newport they leave and Willen see—
A pleasant road with bush and tree,
And Lovat's wave for company.
The Wolstons passed, behold the treen
Of beauteous Woughton-on-the-Green !
The Walton walnuts on the left,
They pass, then swampy Sympson cleft,
Then press they on nor slacken rein
Till Fenny's sleepy town they gain.
Their steeds relinquished, Lovat's fount
They cross, and press towards Brickhill's mount.
Up, up they plod, the crooked village gain
And presently a fairy gorge attain,
With steep and ferny sides, here hare-bells fine,
And, high above, impending shafts of pine.

* A field near.
1 Emberton Tower now occupies this site.
2 Sherington Church.

LXXVIII.

And now within the churchyard's lofty ground
They seat themselves upon a thymy mound,
And with elation from this coign they scan
The spacious landscape—turret, barbican,
Wood, field and meadow, village, cloud-flecked sky,
Lay like a picture stretched before their eye.
Then queried Amabel, "Unloose your mind,
Why are you sad? Is Rosmarine unkind?"—
"I know not," answered he. "Forgive me, do,
But were she here to-day, instead of you,
The chances are I could contrive to say
What I have so much longed to many a day.
Are women, cousin, very hard to win?"—
"Some will surrender soon as you begin,
Others take days, some weeks, and even years,
But, prithee cousin, cast aside your fears,
Put on a joyous face, be not o'er cast,
They all, or nearly all, give in at last."—
"But, cousin mine, what would you have me do?"—
"Already, Nicholas, she doats on you."

LXXIX.

"How throbs my heart, and in my ecstasy,
Forgive me, but if only you were she,
I think I could find courage to say three
Small words—and should her pearly eyelids drop,
And should her tears come, I those beads would stop
With warm embraces. They do come, I'm told,
On such occasions (pleasant vision!) hold!
I'd take her hand, her willingness would be
My answer." Fremband closed his eyes to see
More clearly. Scenes like this, closed eyes see best.
To open them he hesitated lest
The pictures should escape. In courtesy
He could not long sit thus. Reluctantly
At last he opened wide his eyes and said:
"Doubtless, by now my father's board is spread,"
But to his great amazement by his side
(He pinched himself, opened his eyes more wide),
Not Amabel, but Rosmarine was seated
Beside him. Archly thereupon she greeted

Her dazed companion. "Pray forgive the ruse,
Ladies, small tricks may play, with some excuse.
Within the church, just now, I saw you; there
Waits Amabel, to her let both repair."

LXXX.

"Not, Rosmarine, until, thy latticed ear,
(Oh lady, unto me 'bove all things dear),"
Said he, "has heard from me more fervent word,
Than ever lady's shelly ear has heard.
Who flees from battle should be loath to press
His burning suit on girlish loveliness,
But man is always losing, Sweet, or winning,
To lose is not synonymous with sinning ;
He only sins who never strives at all,
Small blame to him who strives and fails should fall.
Some of the noblest lives this world has seen
Have catalogues of blank disasters been,
Yet still the laurel on their head is placed.
Defeated, shattered, they are not disgraced
Who try and try. This thought removes my load,
Bannockburn, Sweet, is but an episode
In a great nation's history. There will be
Yet many a rosier opportunity
For England, dear old England, and for me."

LXXXI.

He took her hand, away it was not drawn,
Beauty did never yet the brave man scorn,
And though fair women, when your brave men sue,
Don't always yield the fort, they often do ;
And Brickhill's height 'tis certain lends a charm
Which causes Beauty somehow to disarm.
What wonder then, considering the intent
Of Fremband, and the fit environment
That Rosmarine (Oh, would that for the space
Of those ten minutes I were in his place !)
Said—nothing, but turned white, then very red,
And sought in vain to hide her shapely head,
For, straight before them, striding up the hill,
Was Reynes her father. Both their hearts stood still,

(I would not, now, had I ten merks to lose,
Be standing in unlucky Fremband's shoes).
And as a moral to adorn my tale—
Better make love in some snug sheltered vale,
Or in a wood, or any place you will,
Rather than high upon a breezy hill.

LXXXII.

But ere Nemesis could distil its gall
A bowery bank it had to pass; withal
Presence of mind in ladies' bosoms sated
With love, to an extent much underrated,
Is present. Whilst the bushes interfered,
Like lightning flash the lady disappeared,
And in her place, like magic spell,
Slipped equally lovely Amabel.
De Reynes, vindictive as a hawk,
Strode swearing up the churchyard walk.
"Why here?" he cried. To his amaze
There met his hot and angry gaze,
Instead of bud-lipped Rosmarine,
     The unexpected Amabel.
     "Lady," he asked, "I pray you tell
Where is that wilful daughter mine."

LXXXIII.

"Soft, soft! Sir knight," said Amabel,
" To speak in wrath you do not well.
Quiet, a moment, please abide,"
(Meantime, young Fremband stept aside)
" Your daughter Rosmarine is near,
And in a twinkling will be here,
And, all my heritage I'll stake,
She loves you dearly for your sake,
And nothing in the world would do,
At all displeasing unto you.
To other matters list a trice
And grant the gift of your advice.
You have not any comments made
On Somery's latest escapade."—
"Nought I have heard."—"Imprimis, then, I'd say,
Your son, dear Ralph, returns this very day."

"God bless you child!"—"He's well and stout."
"Again, God bless you; from that rout
I ne'er expected his return,
And oh, a second Bannockburn,
Fills my old heart with fear and dread,
My much loved Rosmarine has fled."

LXXXIV.

"But listen, I, too, long from strife
To see him home, for I'm his wife."
She knelt.   "Your blessing, sire," she said,
"God's blessings, daughter, on your head."
Her blue sky free from cloud or speck,
Her white arms round the old man's neck
She flung, and then the tale she told
Of Somery fell and Buckingham bold.
"Rogue Somery twice," said he, "has tried
A fall with me I'll tap his pride
Ere many days, I do opine.
But where's my wilful Rosmarine,
I thought I saw her sitting here,
Shrew Fremband's mouth against her ear,
And much relieved I was to see
That it was only you and he.
Were Thomas the one—well it might pass
    For, dear me, I myself was young
    Upon a time, and, madcap, flung
Discretion to the winds—By the mass!
'Tis otherwise with Nicholas,
The younger son. As Thomas is
Your cousin, you could hint, I wis,
When he from war returns that he
Small trouble need expect from me
In case towards my Rosmarine...."—

LXXXV.

"Ah, father, reverend father mine,
Thomas is dead. How many sealed
Their fate upon that mournful field!
And little I like ill news to tell,
But Nicholas," said Amabel,

"Despite your wish is in love...."—"Is't so ?"—
"With Rosmarine, and more, I trow,
In yonder porch they're cooing now,
And a pretty couple they'll make I vow."

LXXXVI.

Sir Ralph, utilitarian,
And blunt, had never been the man
To beat about the bush.   He ran
Towards the porch, and, mentally,
" 'Tis very evident," said he,
" That, Thomas slain, his portion rare
Descends to Nicholas the heir.
It alters the case with Thomas dead."
His old arms very wide outspread,
The lady fair he fondly pressed,
As fathers may do, to his breast.
The dark church had a strange effect on him
After the flaming sun, his eyes were dim,
" My love, you please me," in delight, he cried,
    And in his transport fervently he kissed her.
" Sir knight, I'm won, and I will be your bride—
    Congratulate us if you please, dear sister,"
Exclaimed a voice, and where the knight expected
To see his daughter, with most unaffected
Amazement, he beheld the chaste, but bony
And upright Nichola, arrived from Olney.
Who, judging from his warmth, and words, and carriage,
That she had had an offer clear of marriage,
Had, just as if that moment she'd expected him,
Clinched the whole business promptly, and accepted him.
'Twere better, lost the son, she argued, rather
Than none at all, to take in hand the father,
And to increase the hour's peculiar fitness
Her sister Joan sat hard by as witness,
Whilst from the church there sprang in breathless state
The other sisters to felicitate.

LXXXVII.

De Reynes, who ne'er in strife had feared his man,
Shook like an aspen, and his face turned wan.
In Clifton's fields he'd faced the big wild boar,
But here like craven hound he quailed before

Joan and Anastasia,
Anne, and mincing Nicola.
" You're not the one, no, not the right,"
In desperation, gasped the knight,
" I was looking for...."—" Of course you were,"
Said Joan,—" for me."—" I cannot bear
Your impudence," said disdainful Anne.
" *He* doat on *you*. Could any man !"
And from words, as of yore, the quarrel rose
To scratching, and pulling hair, and blows,
When, taking advantage of the fray,
The gentleman meanly slunk away,
And moralised, " Always observe where you're walking to.
And look in the eye of the person you're talking to,
Don't rush into church like a hoyden at play,
Or the wind on a blustering mid-April day,
Let daughters stay just where their fathers expect them,
For mistakes being made it is hard to correct them."

LXXXVIII.

The gentleman gone, the ladies fair
Dried eye and adjusted their ropy hair,
And far enough recovered to
    Discuss the object of their jaunt,
    In place of verjuice-acting taunt,
When right before their faces, who
Should stand but Amabel. " I know,"
    Said she, " the reason of your coming,
    Prevarication will not do, or mumming,
You came with Nowers and Wellbelow,
To seize and get me in your power,
E'en now they crouch in yonder bower,
But wherefore craft ? why plot and spy ?
You want me, ladies, here am I.
My husband—a courier swift has brought
The news—by your father's men is caught."

LXXXIX.

" Good news, fair news," cried the sisters four,
" Hast any more tidings still in store ?"—
" Good news to you it may likely be,
But oh it's terrible news to me,

And into the dungeon of Olney keep
Your heartless father has thrust him deep,
And bound him fast with chain and thong,
And yet he never did him wrong,
He never—but why should I further say?
I'm here—you take me? Yea or nay?
In Olney vaults my Ralph will be
To vile death done, then Somery
Will work his will and marry me;
If such a course affords you pleasure
I am incapable to measure
Your minds. This done, your fortunes fare
Not unto you but to my heir,
For you it were better, I should infer,
That Somery keep a widower.
However, God will ne'er forsake me,
And if you want me, ladies, take me."
" To whom fair Joan cried in accents tart,
"We think we see through your transparent heart,
For ere we should arrive in yonder hollow,
Fremband and Reynes and many more would follow;
Many ye be, but we are few,
For what could only four and two!
So rather, dear lady, than kidnap you
We'll bid you pleasantly adieu."

XC.

With that mock curtseys low they made,
And just as much of spite displayed
As in such action can be mingled,
Then without loss of time each singled
Her palfrey, and their squires they gain,
The company use spur and rein
And speed away, with none to let* them
And none for certain to regret them.
Their horses felt the keen spurs gore them.

XCI.

But swiftly as they rode, before them
At least a hundred yards ahead,
Another pair of riders sped.

* Hinder.

To know their caste each lady strains
Her eye.   'Twas Fremband and De Reynes.
Ah, how they rode, that frantic pair !
The trees shot by, rude yokels stare
With open mouth, the very wind
They left despairingly behind.
Hamlet and village madly flew,
In Newport they scattered a pedlar Jew
And a group of girls, his hat and pack,
Flew wide, himself upon his back ;
Through Sherington followed a score of dogs,
At Emberton into a herd of hogs
They dashed, nor slackened bit or rein,
Till Clifton's turrets grey they gain.
Straightway King Edward's famous ale
They quaff; their servants in a pail
Bring likewise of that famous brew,
The smoking horses drink it too.

Canto Thirteenth.

The Storming of Olney Castle.

XCII.

REVIVED, De Reynes with shout and rave,
His orders peremptory gave,
And ere five hours of light were sped
To Olney he his followers led,
And on his way, at Ekeney
Joined him a gallant company
Under his kinsman Chamberlain,
Brother to him in Scotland slain.
Through Emberton the concourse tramped,
In Olney street the chargers champed,
Nor slackened any bit or thong
Until before the castle strong
Of Olney ranged to fight they stood.
In those days each man what was good
In his own eyes did, whether love or war,
And each in his own hands took the law,
And cared no more for the king than you
Might care for the Begum of Katmandoo.

Each baron championed his own cause,
There were private sieges, frays, and wars,
And every castellated mound
Became a Thomas Tiddler's ground.

XCIII.

Imprimis De Reynes a trumpet blew,
And when Somery's men to the ramparts flew
He demanded to know what they had done
With Ralph, his well-beloved son,
And swore he would not depart without him.
De Somery nothing knew about him.
Whereat across the bulwarks flew
Expressions stronger than would do
In polished circles. " Archers true,
Shoot," cried De Reynes. The arrows flew.
The archers on each beetling tower,
Returned with interest the shower.
De Reynes's men attempt the moat,
But overturned are raft and boat.
Here venturous churls their ladders plant
Against the wall,—the time was scant
To say a prayer : thrust fiercely down
They drop within the moat and drown.
Then did De Reynes those crackeys bring
 That had in Clifton made such roar.
 Ne'er used were they in siege before.
Big balls of roe-like stone* they fling
Within the castellated ring.
De Somery's men had seen before
Those cannon smoke, and heard them roar,
But deemed that they were only made
Like other wind instruments to be played,
And when philosophers averred
 That they, with effect,
 Round stones could project,
They cackled, and said 'twas absurd.

* Oolite. Olney is built on the oolite (Gr, o-on an egg, so called from its resemblance to the roe of a fish.)

XCIV.

Like apples in autumn, when boys rock the tree,
Or Æolus sets his imprisoned winds free,
The balls dropped about the De Somery ears,
And smashed in his turrets, and silenced his jeers.
Like hail the arrows flew; and spear,
And axe, and other soldiering gear
Flashed in the sun. By uncommon luck
An arrow in Somery's midriff stuck,
And when his men with lightning eye
Perceived their castellan must die
Without ado they raised the grated
Portcullis, and capitulated.
In, like a dammed-up river, poured,
With shout and cry, De Reynes's horde.
Up from the dungeon strong arms drew
The prisoner. How the father flew
His boy, so long lost, to embrace.
The lookers on enlarged the space,
And many a sympathetic tear
Enchannelled rugous cheeks and sear.

XCV.

" Father, benevolent and dear,"
Cried Ralph, " Oh, where is Amabel ?
As you love me, ease my mind and tell."
Just then towards the barbican,
    Two ladies rode. " 'Tis Rosmarine,
    And Amabel, thy love and mine,"
Cried Fremband. Swift those lovers ran,
And midst the heaps of torn and dead,
And broken shafts, and runnels red,
The happy pairs embraced and shed
Such tears as never can be seen
Save when dear friends have sundered been
For months whilst sands but slowly ran,
Or obstacles gargantuan
Have been removed. Loomed then the white,
Thin figure of the eremite.
In cowl, and scapular, and zone,
Who all those years had dwelt alone,
And as he strode the shout out-rung :
" The eremite of Hermit's Tongue ! "

XCVI.

"My children," cried the aged man,
 "For twenty cycles I have spread,
 In yonder solitude my bed,
But God hath now removed my ban.
No longer need I shelter prone
In den with rank growths over-grown
Like cub of wolf or fox. This zone
Is useless too. Need now is none
I wot, sirs, to Beware of one.
Who am I? Amabel you see
A father—your own sire in me."
"My sire," cried Amabel, "is dead."—
"Attend, my child," the old man said,
"The fiend, whose flag this pile displayed,
Whose hests these rogues and knaves obeyed,
With land-greed urged, in company
With others, my brave folk and me.
Attacked—I bore a title then
And owned a castle, lands and men ;
Ye stare, I was—I am again—
Good friends, Sir Richard Chamberlayne.
But wait—my servants all were slain,
And me likewise they left for dead.
 My sense returned, I crawled away
At night. Alas! my reason fled.
 I could not think, I could not pray,
But bit by bit the past returned,
My house and all its stores were burned,
My daughter kidnapped. Turned my hair
To snow—I raved in my despair;
(Ah, how I raved!)—but none believed
My tale. 'Poor man, he is deceived,'
They said, and well they might, for I
For six long years had wandered up
And down the land. Said I : 'His cup
Will some day fill. Then let me die;
Till then no more will I declare,
My name, but low in fox's lair
Or badger's will lie down. In prayer
My days shall pass; and if I can
Do good, I will, to any man ;'"

And so, a priest, I dwelt among
The reeds and flags of Hermit's Tongue

XCVII.

" How oft, my daughter, when you sought
My hut, and evil tidings brought
Of Somery, I longed to tell
My story in my sheltered dell.
How often to my yearning breast
Could I my darling girl have pressed ;
But you, the ward of Somery,
Were one day, too, his wife to be.
However, when I wedded you
To Ralph, from reach, his quarry flew.
But on a prostrate foe one need
Not trample, or exult indeed-
And triumph. Shall the vanished fleck
Our present ! "   Round the old man's neck
She flung her arms ; her frangipane-[1]
Sweet lips again and yet again
She pressed on his, whilst farther stepped
The churls, and many a war-dog wept.
Attention—nor too soon—was then
To stricken Somery paid. His men
Bawled for a leech who directed a wench
To cook on the spur of the moment a drench[2]
Of brier shoots, and oak wood, and ginger, and betony
And sugar (first cautioning lest she should eat any),
    Agrimony sweet, beside,
    Heads of dandelions dried,
The which with the requisite spoonful of yeast
Gives a drench fit to offer a king at a feast,
To say nought of a wicked old bully and tricker
On whom it seemed sinful to waste such good liquor.
But while it was bubbling De Somery died,
And they dug a great hole, very long, deep, and wide,
And emptied him in, with his broad sword of Milan—
And the world was well rid of a specious, old villain.

---

1 Frangipane was a pasty made of cream, sugar, and almonds.
2 This is the receipt for Buckinghamshire " Dire-drink."

XCVIII.

And as for the castle of Olney town
De Reynes and his merry men tore it down,
(For noble or peasant they cared not a groat),
Applying the rubbish to fill up the moat.
The ashlar has since produced farmsteads a few,
And out of it likewise some cottages grew;
And now of the castle remains not a stone,
And the most to be got is a tooth or a bone,
Or a fragment of sword, though of tusks of the boar,
You can find, if you take but the trouble, galore.
But though old De Somery's body was dead
His soul could not rest for the blood he had shed,
And his ghost still at midnight forsakes its abode
And staggers about in the neighbouring Road.
And if you imagine that someone is tricking,
Just see if well into his midriff is sticking
A good cloth yard arrow.   But those who prefer
To avoid him, from home had much better not stir.

Canto Fourteenth.

Reformation.

XCIX.

Six months and a day from the notable fight,
A bridal with everything smiling and bright
Took place in the old church at Clifton ; the pair
United were Fremband and Rosmarine fair ;
And among the guests invited were
The sisters four, but to infer
That the invitation was declined
Betrays a strikingly shallow mind,
For ne'er was lady yet invited
Who bridal invitation slighted.
They went not to bless but to utter malicious
Remarks, and make jibes.   The cates were delicious,
There were pasties of doe, and apricots juicy,
And melons from Spain, sweet, melting, and sluicy;
But for making the water arise to the mouth
There never were apricots sunned in the south

Or melons brought over in yellow-oar'd ships
One half so effective as Rosmarine's lips.
And yet the remarks that the sisters let fall
Concerning those cates, to say nothing at all
Of other amenities, well might arouse
The ire of a celibate pinioned by vows.
But without e'en a word, bright Rosmarine flew
To Joan, and, round her, her chiselled arms threw,
Whose whiteness on Joan's poor yellow neck shone
Like newly dropped snow a foul causeway upon ;
And so warmly she kissed her—so kindly she spoke—
That the pitiful casket round Joan's heart broke,
And the jewel dropped out, " O Rosmarine, dear,
Forgive me, I am the most hateful wretch here."—
" Nay, nay," came reply, and according to plan
That moment sweet Amabel fastened on Anne,
With words just as kind, whose object and trend
Was to change her companion from foe into friend.
But spite of her manner seductive, she failed,
But, a week or two after, again she assailed
Her victim, and with such persuasion she spoke
The thaw came at last; and the solid ice broke.
But Nichola did not relinquish the fray
Till autumn and winter had glided away.
Anastasia took just a year and a day.
But at last all were won, for kindness is catching ;
They gave up their vices, beginning with scratching,
Then scolding, and fibs ; no longer they gnawed
Their nails, and backbiting went too by the board.
But though they were vastly improved in the main,
Control absolute o'er their tempers to gain
Took months.   Even then, on occasion, no doubt
When a bit off their guard the old Adam leaked out.
And then, as their faces grew less and less-sour,
They seemed better looking to get every hour.
As for Nichola, no one in Clifton or Olney·
Considered her now either rufous or bony,
And no one found fault with her rich auburn hair,
And her figure seemed really quite graceful tho' spare,
And Anne—as to warts Astronomy teaches
The sun has its spots—there are specks upon peaches,
And none made remark.   Anastasia's back
Seemed not, after all, very humpy.   No lack

Of champions now did brief Joan enthrall,
And in shoes with high heels she appeared almost tall.
To each came a lover—for short girls and spare ones
Are as much in request as the tall ones and fair ones,
And even a slightly curved back or a wart,
Be their owner good tempered stands almost for nought,
And as for red hair, 'tis my evident duty
To say that some thousands account it a beauty.

C.

And all were wed in the self same hour
   In Olney church—a chariot carried them,
   And the Bishop of London came and married them ;
And with glorious will in the fine church tower
The bells rang backward that notable day,
There was ne'er such a High Buck Holiday.
The stocking was thrown by Rosmarine,
   And Amabel's lips kissed the first ruby cup,
   And Nichola's husband, with grace, took it up ;
But Fremband and Ralph came to words o'er their wine
On a delicate subject I'd rather not mention,
However, the quarrel attracted attention,
So the brides, with a blush, compelled to take heed of
   them,
Said both should be sponsors if e'er there was need of
   them.
And yokel and gentle were happy all day,
There was singing, and feasting, and hoydenish play,
And the din of the revelry reaches my ears
O'er the many-arched bridge of five hundred long years,
And I pray God all sour girls the devil may cheat,
And turn, like four others, kind, gentle and sweet:
   Like Joan, and Anastasia,
   Anne, and graceful Nichola.

OLNEY:
OLIVER RATCLIFF,
PRINTER.

www.ingramcontent.com/pod-product-compliance
Lightning Source LLC
Chambersburg PA
CBHW020551270326
41927CB00006B/805